I0019341

Mainframes, Computing on Big Iron

Patrick H. Stakem

© Oct 2014

3rd Edition

15th in the Computer Architecture Series.

Table of contents

Do not fold, spindle, or mutilate!

Introduction

This book covers the topic of mainframe computers, the room-sized units that dominated and defined computing in the 1950's and 1960's. The coverage is of efforts mainly in the United States, although significant efforts in the U.K., Germany, and other countries were also involved.

How did we get where we are? Initially computers were big, unique, heavy mainframes with a dedicated priesthood of programmers and system engineers to keep them running. They were enshrined in specially air conditioned rooms with raised floors and access control. They ran one job at a time, taking punched cards as input, and producing reams of wide green-striped paper output. Data were collected on reels of magnetic tape, or large trays of punched cards. Access to these very expensive resources was necessarily limited. Computing was hard, but the advantages were obvious – we could collect and crunch data like never before, and compute things that would have worn out our slide rules.

I focus here mostly on computers that I have experience with, although I do cover some of the one-off predecessors that lead to the mainframe industry of the 1960's. Thus, this book is not comprehensive. I probably missed your favorite. Not every machine from every manufacturer is discussed.

Computers were built for one of two purposes, business accounting, or scientific calculations. There was also research in the fledgling area of Computer Science, an area not yet well defined. The computers used peripherals from the Unit Record equipment, designed for business data processing. Data were typed on cards, sorted, and printed mechanically. This was a major improvements over the manual method. Herman Hollerith figured this out, and improved the processing of the U. S. Census in 1890. This took 1 year, as opposed to 8 years for the previous census.

Mainframes are still in use in Business and Science. Thet have grown up a lot but gotten smaller and smarter.

Hollerith set up a company based in Georgetown (part of the District of Columbia) on 29th street to manufacturing punched card equipment. There is a plaque on the building which housed the Tabulating Machine Company, later know as IBM.

At the time, business and science were both using mechanical calculators to handle computations. These were little changed over a hundred years or so. The technology base changed from mechanical to relay to tube, and things got faster. The arithmetic system changed from decimal to binary, because the switching elements in electronics were two-state.

The next step was to put a "computer" between the card reader and the printer, and actually crunch the data.

Then, a better idea evolved. Most of the time, the "big iron" was not computing, it was waiting. So, if we could devise a way to profitably use the idle time, we would increase the efficiency of the facility. This lead to the concept of time-sharing. There was a control program whose job it was to juggle the resources so that a useful program was always running. This came along about the time that remote terminals were hooked to the mainframe, to allow access from multiple, different locations. In a sense, the computer facility was virtualized; each user saw his very own machine (well, for limited periods of time, anyway). If the overhead of switching among users was not too great, the scheme worked.

This evolved into a "client-server" architecture, in which the remote clients had some compute and storage capability of their own, but still relied on the big server.

And, in the background, something else amazing was happening. Mainframes were built from relays and vacuum tubes, magnetic core memory, and massive rotating magnetic drums for storage. These machines, then, with massive card decks of programs and data, were used to design integrated circuits. Eventually, these devices became dominant. Semiconductor technology scales nicely. In fact, Gordon Moore of Intel formulated his famous law from observations that the complexity of the devices doubled every 18 months. This is an exponential growth curve. If we have 1 unit of memory in a package for a certain cost, in 18 months we will have 2 units of memory in the same package for the same price. In 18 more months, 4 units, and so on.

A modern measure of complexity is the number of logic gates per device. A gate is a logic unit built from the underlying technology, be it relay, vacuum tube, or transistor. A single vacuum tube or transistor, with some additional circuitry, can implement a logic gate. The current state-of-the-art is several billion (10^9) gates per device. Two active devices (transistors, vacuum tubes) plus some passive devices (resistors, capacitors) are needed to built a flip-flop, a two-state device for temporary storage of 1 bit of data. It doesn't take long for this to really add up. And, the technology feeds on itself. The computers used to design and manufacture chips keep getting more and more capable.

Now, our phones have orders-of-magnitude more compute and storage capability than any mainframe. My tablet has more capability than my entire University had when I was an undergraduate. Such exponential growth laws can't be sustained forever, but so far, so good.

Mainframes are still in use, but they've gotten slimmer. There are probably more in use today that ever. Now, one thing that mainframes did well was managing large databases of important data. Not just Government data such as tax information, social security records, and Veterans affairs, but commercial data, banking, insurance, credit card accounts, medical data. For a lot of reasons, including security, this should be hosted at one place (with two other places as backup). This brings us back to a client-server model. But technology has marched on, and the mainframe has mostly been replaced with racks of "servers." These machines are pretty much what you have on your desk, minus the keyboard and monitor. They have massive amounts of disk storage, and maybe access to robotic optical media libraries.

If you want to experience running any of the architectures, check out the Software for Simulation of Historical Computers (SIMH) at http://simh.trailing-edge.com/ . The software is available in source, and Windows executables.

NASA retired its last mainframe in 2012.

And take this to heart: *Never trust a computer you can lift.*

Author

The author's first computer experience was on a Bendix G-20 mainframe, a 32-bit machine, using the Algol language. His first assembly language was on an IBM S/360 mainframe, specifically the Model 67 variant, with virtual memory. He went on to program the Univac 1108 series mainframe (a 1's complement machine), the DEC PDP-8, 9, 10, and 11, the Bendix G-15, the Athena Missile Guidance Computer by Sperry Rand and many more. The concept of a personal computer was, at the time, ludicrous.

The author is fairly conversant with IBM Fortra -G and -H, S/360 assembly language, S/360 JCL, Univac Fortran-V, and Bendix G-20 Algol.

In spite of all the interesting computers, the author managed to graduate from Carnegie Mellon University with a BSEE. He went on to get Masters degrees from the Johns Hopkins University in Physics and Computer Science. In the latter area, he never had to write a program. Although, at the time, registration for courses involved getting punched cards by mail, that had to be hand carried back to the main campus to complete registration.

He went on to work as a NASA contractor for 42 years, visiting all of the NASA Centers and launch sites. He specialized in support of spacecraft onboard computers, which was accomplished on mainframes. He "retired" and is taught for the Johns Hopkins University, Engineering for Professionals Program, the Computer Science Department of Loyola University in Maryland, and Capitol Technology University.

Photo Credits

Photos are from the author's collection, unless otherwise noted.

Overview of Computer Architecture

If you know this stuff, or find it boring, skip ahead.

All the mainframes of interest had settled on the binary systems, although some predecessor machines did do decimal math. A bit is the smallest unit of binary information. It represents a yes/no, on/off, left/right type of decision. It can be represented in mathematics as the digits zero or one. Any technology that can represent two distinguishable states can represent a bit. Red light/green light, voltage or no voltage, current or no current, light or darkness, north magnetic or south magnetic, etc. We have to be careful to distinguish between the mathematical concept of a bit (one of two possible states) and its implementation.

A positional number system allows us to choose a base number, and use the digit positions to represent different orders of magnitude, even fractions. In Roman numerals, we have a specific symbol for fifty, and that is L. In decimal, we use 50. That is to say, 5 x 10 (the base) plus 0 times 1.

A computer performs arithmetic and logic functions on data, and provides flow of control. Let's take these one at a time. The arithmetic functions we would like to have performed are additional, subtraction, multiplication, and division. Actually, as we will see later, if we can subtract, we can do any of these operations. Multiplication is merely repeated addition. The logical operations on binary data include inversion, AND, OR, Exclusive OR, and derivative functions such as Negated-AND (NAND), Negated-OR (NOR), and Negated-Exclusive OR (NXOR). Actually, for two binary symbols, there are 16 possible functions. Only some of these have names (and are useful). As with the mathematical functions, some can be represented as combinations of others. We'll look at mathematical and logical functions applied to binary data, and how the mathematical functions can be expressed in terms of the logical ones.

IBM was 2's comp, Univac was 1's comp. IBM used base-16 hexadecimal, Univac used base-8 (octal).

Integers

All the numbers we talk about will be integers (until we get to floating point). Integers have a finite range. Eight bits gives us 256 (2^8) numbers, and 16 bits gives us nearly 65000. We need to give up one bit (or, 1/2 of our range of numbers) for a sign position.

Negative numbers

There are many ways to do represent negative numbers. The case we are familiar with from our use of decimal is the use of a special symbol "-". This gives us the sign-magnitude format.

We could do this in binary as well, and, in addition, there are the 1's complement and 2's complement schemes of representing negative numbers. To form the 1's complement of a binary number, change all bits to their logical complement. Problem is, in a finite (closed) number system, the 1's complement system gives two different representations of zero (ire., +0 and -0), both valid. To form the 2's complement, do the 1's complement and add 1. This is a more complex operation, but the advantage is, there is only one representation of zero. Because zero is considered a positive number, there is one more negative number than positive number in this representation. Two's complement has become the dominant choice for negative number representation in computers.

One's complement was used on the Univac 1108 series mainframes. A problem was that 0 and -0 did not test equal. That can be a problem.

The Von Neumann Architecture says there is no distinction between the code and the data. This was an observation by John Von Neumann of the Institute for Advanced Studies at Princeton University. While consulting for the Moore School of Electrical

Engineering at the University of Pennsylvania, Von Neumann wrote an incomplete "First Draft of a Report on the EDVAC" (computer). The paper described a computer architecture in which the data and the program are both stored in the computer's memory in the same address space. Before this, it was the custom to have separate code and data storage (Harvard architecture), and they were not necessarily the same size or format. Von Neumann noted that the code is data. Most modern microprocessors are this style. For speed, especially in digital signal processors, designers revert to the older "Harvard" architecture, with separate code and data stores, as this gives a speed-up in accessing from memory. In a Harvard architecture it is also difficult to have self-modifying code, which is a good thing from the debugging standpoint.

The Instruction Set Architecture (ISA) defines the data types, the instructions, the internal architecture of the CPU, addressing modes, interrupt handling, and input/output. The ISA is defined before implementation of the hardware. It may be legacy, as is the case with the Intel 16-bit ISA, now extended to 64 bit, or the ARM ISA. Many other examples can be found in the computer field, such as the Digital Equipment Corporation VAX, and the IBM System/360.

The ISA defines what the processor does, not how it does it. There are different implementations of the ISA that produce the same results with different methods.

Instruction types in an ISA include data movement and operations on data. Data movement includes operations to input and output data from external devices, move data to and from registers, and to and from memory. Operations on data include the standard mathematical and logical operations. Control flow instructions provide a mechanism for the independent and data-dependent transfer of control. This group includes branches, jumps, loops, subroutine call and return, interrupt vectoring, and system calls.

The instructions can provide additional features, such as block moves, stack operations, or an atomic test and set. This latter instruction helps implementing coordination among multiple processes, using a mutual exclusion property.

An instruction consists of several parts, the op code, and the operands. The op code is usually the leftmost part of the instruction, the first to be fetched, and thus allowing for the decoding process to begin as the operands are fetched. There may be zero, one, two, three, or more operands. The standard logical or mathematical operation is a function of two (input) variables, and produces a single output.

Binary Coded Decimal uses 10 of the possible 16 codes in 4 bits. The other bit patterns are not used, or could be used to indicate sign, error, overflow, or such. BCD converts to decimal easily, and provides a precise representation of decimal numbers. It requires serial by digit calculations, but gives exact results. It uses more storage than binary integers, and the implementation of the logic for operations is a bit more complex. It is an alternative to the limited range or precision of binary integers, and the complexity of floating point. BCD is used extensively in instrumentation and personal calculators. Support for operations on BCD numbers were provided in the IBM mainframes.

BCD 4 bit code, only 10 valid values:

0000 = 0   0001 = 1   0010 = 2   0011 = 3

0100 = 4

0101 = 5   0110 = 6   0111 = 7   1000 = 8

1001 = 9

1010, 1011, 1100, 1101, 1110, 1111 = invalid number codes in BCD

BCD numbers (4 bits) can be stored in a byte, which uses more storage, but makes calculations easier. These are sometimes referred to as BCD nibbles. Alternately, BCD digits can be packed 2 to a byte.

Arithmetic operations in BCD format numbers are usually done in binary, and then adjusted to handle the carry (or borrow). For example, in packed BCD, we may generate a carry between the 3rd and 4th bit position. Subtraction is usually implemented by adding the 10's complement of the subtrahend. The 10's complement is formed by taking the 9's complement, and then adding one. The 9's complement can be formed by subtracting the digits from 9. If a BCD arithmetic operation generates an invalid BCD result, 6 can be added to force a carry. BCD strings of numbers can have a "decimal point" inserted wherever convenient. Additional bookkeeping is then needed to keep the numbers commensurate for addition and subtraction, and to adjust in multiplication and division.

ASCII Format

American Standard Code for Information Interchange (ASCII) was devised for communication of symbols for teletypes from the 1960's. It is a 7-bit code with 128 combinations. This gives us four groups of 32: control, lower case, upper case, numbers and punctuation characters. An ASCII character fits in an 8-bit byte, with one bit to spare. This is sometimes used as a parity bit, for error control. At the time, paper tape systems supported 8 bits. Later, support was included in 9-track, reel-to-reel tape and punch cards.

Although a 7-bit code can handle the Roman alphabet, upper and lower case, numbers, punctuation, and control characters, it is not useful for character systems (such as Amharic) that have a large number of letter combinations, or logosyllabic systems such as Chinese. ASCII extensions address variations in Latin letters, such as those found in Italian, Spanish, Portuguese, French, and other Latin based languages, and regional uses, such as the British Pound sign (for currency), represented on US keyboards as "#".

Earlier codes, such as the 5-bit Baudot code (circa 1870), used a *shift* mechanism to allow additional codes. The term "baud," referring to the symbol rate of transmission of information, is named for Emile Baudot, the originator of the code. Baud rate is not necessarily the same as bit rate; it depends on how many bits it takes to represent a symbol (such as a Baudot or ASCII character). Baudot code was used well into the 20th century for teleprinter equipment, particularly on the AT&T TWX network.

An Escape sequence is initiated by a special code, the Escape character (ESC). This defines the following characters to be control characters, not encoded numbers or digits, until a second ESC is received. This is contrasted with control characters, that have defined functions, such as tab or carriage return (which is a typewriter term). The ESC key is still included on keyboards. Control characters usually have no displayed equivalent.

ASCII's heritage in teletype machines sometimes causes confusion in modern data communications. For example, teletypes needed both a carriage return (CR) and a line feed (LF) at the end of a line. Non-mechanical systems can do both operations with just a CR. The Bell character, designed to ring the Teletype's bell at the receiving end for attention (or annoyance) has no parallels. The Backspace character was used to back up paper tape to overwrite errors. ASCII is defined to be transmitted least significant bit first.

The Central Processing Unit

A computer performs arithmetic and logic functions on data, and provides flow of control. Let's take these one at a time. The arithmetic functions we would like to have performed are additional, subtraction, multiplication, and division. Actually, as we will see later, if we can subtract, we can do any of these operations. The logical operations on binary data include inversion, AND, OR, Exclusive OR, and derivative functions such as Negated-AND (NAND), Negated-OR (NOR), and Negated-Exclusive OR (NXOR). As with the mathematical functions, some can be represented as combinations of others. We look at mathematical and logical functions applied to binary data, and how the mathematical functions can be expressed in terms of the logical ones.

Input/Output

Input/Output (I/O) provides a user interface, and a link between systems. The basic I/O methods of polled, interrupt, and dma are supported by the cpu chips, but additional support chips are required to implement these functions. There are many options. We will consider the specific implementation of the IBM pc circuit board, which has evolved into an industry standard architecture.

I/O Methods

Regardless how bits or signals come to a computer, there are several standards methods to sample them, or send them out. The various communication protocols define the physical connection (connectors) and electrical interface (voltages, etc.). Once we are at the processor chip boundary, and we are dealing with bits, there are three common schemes to read or write. These can be implemented in hardware or software. The three schemes are polled I/O, interrupts, or direct memory access. All of these schemes work with serial (bit-at-a-time) or parallel (many-bits-at-a-time) I/O.

There are three basic methods for I/O implementation, polled I/O, interrupts, and direct memory access.

Polled I/O

In polled I/O, the computer periodically checks to see if data is available, or if the communications channel is ready to accept new output. This is somewhat like checking your phone every few seconds to see if anyone is calling. There's a more efficient way to do it, which we'll discuss next, but you may not have anything better to do. Polled I/O is the simplest method. Specific I/O instructions are provided in the Intel processors. Both serial and parallel interfaces are used on the IBM pc board level architecture.

Interrupt

In Interrupt I/O, when a new piece of information arrives, or the communication channel is ready to accept new output, a control signal called an interrupt occurs. This is like the phone ringing. You are sitting at your desk, busy at something, and the phone rings, interrupting you, causing you to set aside what you are doing, and handle the new task. When that is done, you go back to what you were doing. A special piece of software called an interrupt service routine is required. At this point, the phone rings....

Control transfer mechanism, somewhat like a subroutine call, but can be triggered by an external event. External events can make a request for service. The Intel cpu architecture supports 256 levels of interrupt, with a single interrupt line. The specific interrupt number is put on the cpu data bus, in the lower 8-bits. This requires one or more external interrupt prioritization chips. The IBM pc architecture uses 8 levels of interrupt, and the later IBM AT architecture supports 15.

There are hardware interrupts, defined by the architecture of the cpu and the motherboard it resides on. These interrupts are triggered by events external to the cpu, and are thus asynchronous to its operation

We can get the same effect by executing software interrupt commands. This provides a convenient mechanism for a user program to call the Operating System and request services. There interrupts are synchronous.

Exceptions are interrupts caused in response to a condition encountered during execution of an instruction. For example, an attempted division by zero would trigger an exception. These are also synchronous interrupts.

External Interrupts are asynchronous to the CPU's operation. It is hard to duplicate their timing. There are implications for debugging multiple interrupt systems in a real-time environment. We need to know the state of the machine, at every instant of time.

DMA

Direct Memory access is the fastest way to input or output information. It does this directly to or from memory, without processor intervention.

Let's say we want to transmit a series of 32-bit words. The processor would have to fetch this word from memory, send it to the I/O interface, and update a counter. In DMA, the I/O device can interface directly to or from the memory. DMA control hardware includes housekeeping tasks such as keeping a word count, and updating the memory pointer.

DMA also makes use of interrupts. Normally, we load a word count into a register in the DMA controller, and it is counted down as words transfer to or from memory. When the word count reaches zero, and interrupt is triggered to the processor to signal the end of the transfer event.

While the DMA is going on, the processor may be locked out of memory access, depending on the memory architecture. Also, if dynamic memory is being used, the processor is usually in charge of memory refresh. This can be handled by the DMA controller, but someone has to do it.

The DMA scheme used on the IBM pc toggles between the CPU and the DMA device on a per-word basis. Thus, the processor is not locked out of fetching and executing instructions during a DMA, although the DMA transfer is not as fast as it could be.

Also, DMA is not constrained to access memory linearly; that is a function of the DMA controller and its complexity. For example, the DMA controller can be set up to access every fourth word in memory.

The DMA protocol uses a Request and Grant mechanism. The device desiring to use dma send a request to the cpu, and that request is granted when the cpu is able. This is similar to the interrupt request for service mechanism. A dma controller interfaces with the device and the cpu. It may handle multiple dma channels with differing priorities. The controller has to know, for each request, the starting address in memory, and the size of the data movement. For dma data coming in to ram, there is the additional complication of updating cache.

During the dma transfer, the dma controller takes over certain tasks from the cpu. This includes updating the memory address, and keeping track of the word count. The word count normally goes to zero, and generates an interrupt to signal the cpu that the dma transfer is over. The cpu can continue execution, as long as it has code and data available.

Serial versus parallel

A bus architecture is used as a short-distance parallel communications pathway between functional elements, such as the cpu and memory. The length of parallel signal lines is severely restricted by bit skew, where all the bits don't get to a particular point at the same time. This is due in some part by the differing characteristics of the circuit board traces implementing the bus. Each path must be treated as a transmission line at the frequencies involved, and have balanced characteristics with all the other lines, and be properly terminated.

The fetch/execute cycle

This section discusses how an instruction gets executed. The basic process is referred to as the fetch/execute cycle. First the instruction is fetched from memory, then the instruction is executed, which can involve the fetching and writing of data items, as well as mathematical and logical operations on the data.

Instructions are executed in steps called machine cycles. Each machine cycle might take several machine clock times to complete. If the architecture is pipelined, then each machine cycle consists of a stage in the pipeline. At each step, a memory access or an internal operation (ALU operation) is performed. Machine cycles are sequenced by a state machine in the cpu logic. A clock signal keeps everything going in lockstep.

A register called the program counter holds a pointer to the location in memory of the next instruction to be executed. At initialization (boot), the program counter is loaded with the location of the first instruction to be executed. After that, the program counter is simply incremented, unless there is a change in the flow of control, such as a branch or jump. In this case, the target address of the branch or jump is put into the program counter.

The first step of the instruction execution is to fetch the instruction from memory. It goes into a special holding location called the Instruction Register. At this point the instruction is decoded, meaning a control unit figures out, from the bit pattern, what the instruction is to do. This control unit implements the ISA, the instruction set architecture. Without getting too complicated, we could have a flexible control unit that could execute different ISA's. That's possible, but beyond the scope of our discussion here.

The instruction decode complete, the machine knows what resources are required for instruction execution. A typical math instruction, for example, would require two data reads from memory, an ALU operation, and a data write. The data items might be in registers, or memory. If the instruction stream is regular, we can pipeline the operation. We have stages in the pipeline for instruction fetch, instruction decode, operand(s) read, ALU operation, and operand write. If we have a long string of math operations, at some point, each stage in the pipeline is busy, and an instruction is completed at each clock cycle. But, if a particular instruction requires the result of a previous instruction as an input, the scheme falls apart, and the pipeline stalls. This is called a dependency, and can be addressed by the compiler optimizing the code by re-ordering. This doesn't always work. When a change in the flow of control occurs (branch, jump, interrupt), the pipeline has to be flushed out and refilled. On the average, the pipeline speeds up the process of executing instructions.

A special purpose hardware device, purpose-built, will always be faster than a general purpose device programmed or configured for a specific task. This means that purpose-built hardware is the best, yet least flexible choice. Programmability provides flexibility, and reduces the cost of change. A new approach, provided by

Field Programmable Gate Array (FPGA) technology, gives us the ability to reconfigure the hardware and well as the software. That discussion is beyond the scope of this book.

Floating Point

This section describes the floating point number representation, and explains when it is used, and why. Floating point is an old computer technique for gaining dynamic range in scientific and engineering calculations, at the cost of accuracy. First, we look at fixed point, or integer, calculations to see where the limitations are. Then, we'll examine how floating point helps expand the limits.

In a finite word length machine, there is a tradeoff between dynamic range and accuracy in representation. The value of the most significant bit sets the dynamic range because the effective value of the most positive number is infinity. The value of the least significant bit sets the accuracy, because a value less than the LSB is zero. And, the MSB and the LSB are related by the word length.

In any fixed point machine, the number system is of a finite size. For example, in 18 bit word, we can represent the positive integers from 0 to 2^{18}-1, or 262,143. A word of all zeros = 0, and a word of all ones = 262,143. I'm using 18 bits as an example because it's not too common. There's nothing magic about 8, 16, or 32 bit word sizes.

If we want to use signed numbers, we must give up one bit to represent the sign. Of course, giving up one bit halves the number of values available in the representation. For a signed integer in an 18 bit word, we can represent integers from + to - 131,072. Of course, zero is a valid number. Either the positive range or the negative range must give up a digit so we can represent zero. For now, let's say that in 18 bits, we can represent the integers from -131,072 to 131,071.

There are several ways of using the sign bit for representation. We can have a sign-magnitude format, a 1's complement, or a two's complement representation. Most computers use the 2's complement representation. This is easy to implement in hardware. In this format, to form the negative of a number, complement all of the bits (1->0, 0->1), and add 1 to the least significant bit position. This is equivalent to forming the 1's complement, and then adding one. One's complement format has the problem that there are two representations of zero, all bits 0 and all bits 1. The hardware has to know that these are equivalent. This added complexity has led to 1's complement schemes falling out of use in favor of 2's complement. In two's complement, there is one representation of zero (all bits zero), and one less positive number, than the negatives. (Actually, since zero is considered positive, there are the same number. But, the negative numbers have more range.) This is easily illustrated for 3-bit numbers, and can be extrapolated to any other fixed length representation.

Remember that the difference between a signed and an unsigned number lies in our interpretation of the bit pattern.

Up to this point we have considered the bit patterns to represent integer values, but we can also insert an arbitrary binary point (analogous to the decimal point) in the word. For integer representations, we have assumed the binary point to lie at the right side of the word, below the LSB. This gives the LSB a weight of 2^0, or 1, and the msb has a weight of 2^{16}. (The sign bit is in the 2^{17} position). Similarly, we can use a fractional representation where the binary point is assumed to lie between the sign bit and the MSB, the MSB has a weight of 2^{-1}, and the LSB has a weight of 2^{-17}. For these two cases we have:

The MSB sets the range, the LSB sets the accuracy, and the LSB and MSB are related by the word length. For cases between these extremes, the binary point can lie anywhere in the word, or for that matter, outside the word. For example, if the binary point is assumed to lie 2 bits to the right of the LSB, the LSB weight, and thus the precision, is 2^2. The MSB is then 2^{19}. We have gained dynamic range at the cost of precision. If we assume the binary point is to the left of the MSB, we must be careful to ignore the sign, which does not have an associated digit weight. For an assumed binary point 2 bit positions to the right of the MSB, we have a MSB weight of 2^{-3}, and an LSB weight of 2^{-20}. We have gained precision at the cost of dynamic range.

It is important to remember that the computer does not care where we assume the binary point to be. It simply treats the numbers as integers during calculations. We overlay the bit weights and the meanings.

A 16-bit integer can represent the values between -16384 to 16384

A 32-bit integer can represent the values between $-2*10^9$ to $2*10^9$

A short real number has the range 10^{-37} to 10^{38} in 32 bits.

A long real number has the range 10^{-307} to 10^{308} in 64 bits

We can get 18 decimal (BCD) digits packed into 80 bits.

To add or subtract scaled values, they must have the same scaling factor; they must be commensurate. If the larger number is normalized, the smaller number must be shifted to align it for the operation. This may have the net result of adding or subtracting zero, as bits fall out the right side of the small word. This is like saying that 10 billion + .00001 is approximately 10 billion, to 13 decimal places of accuracy.

In multiplication, the scaling factor of the result is the sum of the scaling factors of the products. This is analogous to engineering notation, where we learn to add the powers of 10.

In division, the scaling factor of the result is the difference between the scaling factor of the dividend and the scaling factor of the divisor. The scaling factor of the remainder is that of the dividend. In engineering notation, we subtract the powers of 10 for a division.

In a normal form for a signed integer, the most significant bit is one. This says, in essence, that all leading zeros have been squeezed out of the number. The sign bit does not take part in this procedure. However, note that if we know that the most significant bit is always a one, there is no reason to store it. This gives us a free bit in a sense; the most significant bit is a 1 by definition, and the msb-1-th bit is adjacent to the sign bit. This simple trick has doubled the effective accuracy of the word, because each bit position is a factor of two.

The primary operation that will cause a loss of precision or accuracy is the subtraction of two numbers that have nearly but not quite identical values. This is commonly encountered in digital filters, for example, where successive readings are differenced. For an 18 bit word, if the readings differ in, say, the 19th bit position, then the difference will be seen to be zero. On the other hand, the scaling factor of the parameters must allow sufficient range to hold the largest number expected. Care must be taken in subtracting values known to be nearly identical. Precision can be retained by pre-normalization of the arguments.

During an arithmetic operation, if the result is a value larger than the greatest positive value for a particular format, or less than the most negative, then the operation has overflowed the format. Normally, the absolute value function cannot overflow, with the exception of the absolute value of the least negative number, which has no corresponding positive representation, because we made room for the representation of zero.

In addition, the scaling factor can increase by one, if we consider the possibility of adding two of the largest possible numbers. We can also consider subtracting the largest (absolute value) negative number from the largest (in an absolute sense) negative number.

A one bit position left shift is equivalent to multiplying by two. Thus, after a one position shift, the scaling factor must be adjusted to reflect the new position of the binary point. Similarly, a one bit position right shift is equivalent to division by two, and the scaling factor must be similarly adjusted after the operation.

Numeric overflow occurs when a nonzero result of an arithmetic operation is too small in absolute value to be represented. The result is usually reported as zero. The subtraction case discussed above is one example. Taking the reciprocal of the largest positive number is another.

As in the decimal representation, some numbers cannot be represented exactly in binary, regardless of the precision. Non-terminating fractions such as 1/3 are one case, and the irrational numbers such as e and pi are another. Operations involving these will result in inexact results, regardless of the format. However, this is not necessarily an error. The irrationals, by definition, cannot exactly be represented by a ratio of integers. Even in base 10 notation, e and pi extend indefinitely.

When the results of a calculation do not fix within the format, we must throw something away. We normally delete bits from the right (or low side) side of the word (the precision end). There are several ways to do this. If we simply ignore the bits that won't fit within the format, we are truncating, or rounding toward zero. We choose the closest word within the format to represent the results. We can also round up by adding 1 to the LSB of the resultant word if the first bit we're going to throw away is a 1. We can also choose to round to even, round to odd, round to nearest, round towards zero, round towards + infinity, or round towards - infinity. Consistency is the desired feature.

If we look at typical physical constants, we can get some idea of the dynamic range that we'll require for typical applications. The mass of an electron, you recall, is 9.1085 x 10-^{31} grams. Avogadro's number is 6.023 x 10^{23}. If we want to multiply these quantities, we need a dynamic range of $10^{(23+31)} = 10^{54}$, which would require a 180 bit word (10^{54} approx.= 2^{180}). Most of the bits in this 180 bit word would be zeros as place holders. Well, since zeros don't mean anything, can't we get rid of them? Of course.

We need dynamic range, and we need precision, but we usually don't need them simultaneously. The floating point data structure will give us dynamic range, at the cost of being unable to exactly represent data.

So, finally, we talk about floating point. In essence, we need a format for the computer to work with that is analogous to engineering notation, a mantissa and a power of ten. The two parts of the word, with their associated signs, will take part in calculation exactly like the scaled integers discussed previously. The exponent is the scaling factor that we used. Whereas in scaled integers, we had a fixed scaling factor, in floating point, we allow the scaling factor to be carried along with the word, and to change as the calculations proceed.

The representation of a number in floating point, like the representation in scientific notation, is not unique. For example,

$$6.54x\ 10^2 = .654\ x\ 10^3 = 654.\ x\ 10^0$$

In the floating point representation, the number of bits assigned to the exponent determines dynamic range, and the number of bits assigned to the mantissa determine the precision, or resolution. For a fixed word size, we must allocate the available bits between the precision (mantissa), and the range (exponent).

Granularity is defined as the difference between representable numbers. This term is normally equal to the absolute precision, and relates to the least significant bit.

There is a use for numbers that are not in normal form, so-called de-normals. This has to do with decreasing granularity, and the fact that numbers in the range between zero and the smallest normal number. A denorm has an exponent which is the smallest representable exponent, with a leading digit of the mantissa not equal to zero. An un-normalized number, on the other hand, has the same mantissa case, but an exponent which is not the smallest representable. Let's get back to engineering...

If the result of an operation results in a number too large (in an absolute magnitude case) to be represented, we have generated an overflow. If the result is too small to be represented, we have an underflow. Results of an overflow can be reported as infinity (+ or - as required), or as an error bit pattern. The underflow case is where we have generated a denormalized number. The IEEE standard, discussed below, handles denorms as valid operands. Another approach is to specify resultant denorms as zero.

There are many standards for the floating point representation, with the IEEE standard now being the defacto industry choice. Before that, manufacturers made their own floating point standards, not just in how the numbers were represented, by how rounding and truncation was handled. And, these were not consistent. IBM had at least two floating point standards in Fortran.

Technologies

This section discusses the technologies used to implement large computing machines, and some of the evolution of that technology.

Logic elements

A relay is an electromechanical switch. Applying voltage to the coil closes the switch. Relays can be connected in series or parallel, giving us the AND and OR logical functions. The relay can also be configured to implement the Logical NOT function. Relays can have multiple independent contacts, and multiple positions. Relays were used to implement early telephone exchanges, and for railroad signaling. Relays are not particularly fast, and they dissipate a lot of power, particularly if they need to be energized to maintain a state (position).

Logical operations are done on a bit-by-bit basis. There is no interaction between adjacent bit positions. The Unary function, (function of 1 variable) is "negate". This changes a 0 to a 1, or a 1 to a 0. there is one input, and one output. That can be done with one relay, one tube, or 1 transistor.

There are 16 possible binary functions (function of 2 input variables). These include AND, OR, and XOR, and their negations, NAND, NOR, and NXOR. The other 10 don't have specific names.

These are 16 functions of two input variables: $C = f(A,B)$. some of these are AND, OR, XOR, etc, and their inverses.

Heavy duty power relay. It operates with 12 volts, and the contacts can switch many amps. Relays can be used to store one bit. They can also be used as an inverting logic element.

Vacuum tubes consist of a low voltage heating element and various plates and screens (grids) sealed in a glass or metal container, with a vacuum. The vacuum is necessary for the electron mobility. The heating element produces free electrons, that travel in a single direction, allowing the tube to act like a rectifier or diode. We can place charged grids in the electron flow, and use these as control elements. The British word for tube is valve. It is actually an electrical valve, controlling the flow of electrons. It can operate in an on-off mode for digital logic, or a proportional mode, giving amplification. Tubes date from around 1910.

A typical heater voltage was 6 volts, although this varied with manufacturer and type. Typical voltage across the tube could be 100's of volts, making troubleshooting an adventure. Although, if the tube was not lit up by the filament, you knew it was bad. They got very hot in operation, and were also fragile, limiting their use in mobile equipment. One tube could serve as an on-off switch, or a replacement for a relay. A big problem with tubes was service life, and mean-time-to failure.

Tube from IBM.

Transistors have a tremendous advantage over tubes. They can be built much smaller, dissipate much less heat, and required much less power to operate. Diodes are easy to fabricate, as well as resistors and capacitors. Capacitors can be used for data storage, or we can devise a silicon flip-flop from basic logic gates, implemented in transistors. Putting multiple transistors together on a substrate interconnected into a circuit give us an integrated circuit. At today's state of the art, we can put and interconnect literally billions of transistors on a substrate.

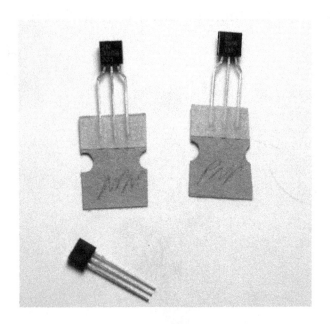

Individual transistors. They come in two flavors, NPN and PNP, depending on how the silicon layers are arranged.

A pair of transistors can be used to build a flip-flop, a logic element storing one bit. A single transistor can form a logic inverter. Coupled with some silicon diodes, we can build logic gates.

When more than 1 transistor at a time could be produced on a single substrate, we could begin to build logic functions on a chip. In small scale integration, only a few gates could be included.

Some logic chips, 16 pin

With medium and large scale integration, we could combine gates into functional units such as Arithmetic logic units (ALU's). Here's how.

We talked about logic functions, and their implementation, but we want to do math. No problem. Here, we see that mathematical functions can be implemented by binary logical operations. That's good, because microelectronics implements logical functions easily. George Boole worked out the theoretical basis of this in the middle 1800's.

Addition

+		half-add	carry	
0	0	0	0	$0 + 0 = 0$
0	1	1	0	$0 + 1 = 1$
1	0	1	0	$1 + 0 = 1$
1	1	0	1	$1 + 1 = 0$, with a carry (this is

like saying, $5 + 5 = 0$, with a carry, in the decimal system)

ADD = half-add (XOR) plus carry (AND)

Similarly, for subtraction

-		half-add	borrow	
0	0	0	0	$0 - 0 = 0$
0	1	1	1	$0 - 1 = 0$, with a borrow
1	0	1	0	$1 - 0 = 0$
1	1	0	0	$1 - 1 = 0$

SUB = half-add (XOR) plus borrow (one of the unnamed functions).

X (times)			multiply
0	0	0	$0 \times 0 = 0$

0	1	0	$0 \times 1 = 0$
1	0	0	$1 \times 0 = 0$
1	1	1	$1 \times 1 = 1$

Multiplication is the AND function.

Division

0	0	not allowed operation	$0/0$ = not an allowed operation
0	1	0	$0/1 = 0$
1	0	not allowed operation	$1/0$ = not an allowed operation
1	1	1	$1/1 = 1$

Division is another of the unnamed operations in the earlier table.

Data Storage

Data storage was accomplished in a series of technologies, before solid state memory became dominant, and rotating magnetic disks became common. All-in-all, we have come a long way since computers stored bits as acoustic waves in a pool of mercury. Let me back up this draft on a flash drive, and on the Cloud...

Delay line memory was a type of sequential access memory that was refreshable. The technology is analog based, and dates from the 1920's. The delay line allows us to start a pulse train , and get it back at a known point in the future. The technique for using this in a digital computer was developed in the mid 1940's by J. Prosper Eckert for the EDVAC. A 1953 patent covered a mercury-based delay line by Eckert and Mauchley. Other technologies included an inductor/capacitor delay line, magnetorestrictive technology, and a rotating magnetic disk with the write heads and the read heads separated. Delay lines had been in use in radar units in World War-II. Data were stored acoustically. This could be in columns of mercury. The speed of sound in mercury is 1450 meters/second. The mercury had to be kept at a constant temperature, usually 100 degrees F. The Univac I used mercury delay tubes, each storing 120 bits. The 1000 word store was the size of a small room. The access time was close to 225 microseconds.

Data were also stored as torsional waves in a wire medium. Necessarily, both delay line memory and the torsional wire systems were sequential access, like the later paper or mylar tape drive systems.

CRT's used to store data as electrostaticly charged areas on the face of a glass tube were also used in the 1940's and 1950's. These were mostly implemented with World

War-2 surplus radar displays. Memory location was specified by the X and Y plate voltages applied to the tube. This steered the electron beam to a specific spot on the face. The bit stream modulated the electron beam. As the beam swept across the face of the tube, there were short bright lines and dark spots, representing 1's and 0's. To read the values, the same "address" was fed to the deflection plates, The energy of the electron beam was increased, and when it swept a lit area, many more electrons were emitted than for a blank area. This was read by a metal plate in front of the glass face of the tube. Reading was destructive, but later tubes were made with two electron guns, one for reading and one for writing.

You can also use flip-flops as storage elements, and tube-based flip flops were used as the registers of early machines. It takes two tubes to make a flip-flop, although special purpose tubes with double elements were also developed.

Magnetic core memory dominated the computer field for decades, certainly from the mid 1950's to around the mid 70's. The technology used ferrite beads or toruses, with four wires threaded through them. The cores could be magnetized in one of two directions, and could be (destructively) read out. Because of the destructive read, each read operation needed to be followed by a write operation, if the information was to be maintained. Each core held one bit. Semiconductor memory was smaller, cheaper, used less power, and could be mass-produced. It became the dominant memory technology in the 1970's.

Cores evolved from transformer technology, and used materials with square magnetic hysteresis characteristics. Computer pioneers were applying this in computer memory before the end of World War-2. The cores could also be used to replace relays in digital logic. Cores were faster than vacuum tube based solutions. Cores could also be arranged in a 3-dimensional architecture. The core planes held bits of a word. A 16-bit machine has 16 planes. The Whirlwind machine was the first to get core memory, in 1953.

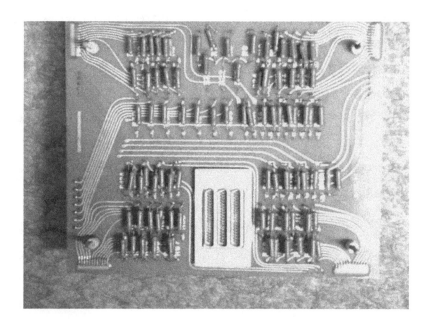

Core module, connections.

Core was manufactured by Fabritek, Ampex, Lockheed, and others. It was a very manual operation to manufactures. In the early days, 4 wires were threaded through the cores by a crew of women with fine motor skills, good at knitting. As cores got physically smaller, this got more challenging. One wire had to be installed at 45 degrees to the rest. Workers needed magnifiers as the cores got smaller.

There were several core configurations, and patents, but the most popular format was the coincident-current. Here there were 4 wires in each core, the X, the Y, the inhibit, and the sense. In a write operation, the core at the junction of the selected X and W wire would be written to, unless the inhibit line was also high. Each X and Y line carried ½ of the current needed to write the bit. The direction of current flow determined the core value, "1" or "0" depending on whether the magnetic filed went clockwise or counterclockwise. Reading is an attempt to flip the core's bit to zero. If that works, it was a one. If not signal is detected, is was already a zero.

Writing a "1" invoked current flow through the X and Y lines in the opposite direction as for a read. To write a zero, the inhibit line carries the amount of current needed to write a bit, but in the opposite direction from the X and

Y (with ½ the current each). Core memory controllers were complicated. Further complications arose because the temperature of the cores was critical. Sometimes, during the boot process, you had to wait a half hour for the core to reach operating temperature. Actual temperature was not as critical as a consistent temperature.

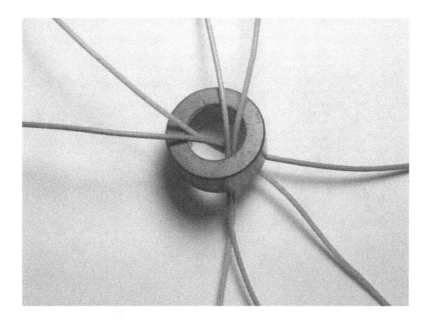

Coincident current wiring for a single core (1 bit).

Core were organized into planes, each plane containing one bit of a word, and as many planes as bits in a word. Core memory had about a 6 microsecond cycle time, improving to under a microsecond by the mid-1970's when semiconductor memory took over. An interesting fact about core memory is that it is non-volatile. For example, the core memory in the Saturn Guidance Computer in the Smithsonian contains the last test program loaded.

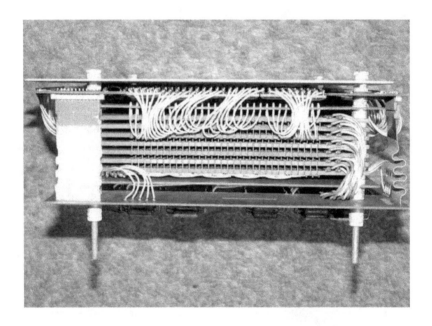

Core module, showing edge-on the planes.

Core persists in MRAM, or magnetorestrictive random access memory chips. They are non-volatile components, produced in integrated circuit technology.

Computer memory is organized in a hierarchy. We would like to have large amounts of low power, fast, non-volatile storage. These requirements are mutually exclusive. The memory closest to the CPU is fast, random-access, volatile, and semiconductor-based, but expensive. Secondary storage, such as disk, is slower, cheaper, persistent, and cheaper on a cost-per-bit basis. Backup storage, offline optical or magnetic, is still cheaper per bit, but may have a longer access time.

In RAM, random access memory, any element is accessible in the same clock time, as opposed to sequential media, such a tape or a disk. In sequential media, the access time varies, and depends on the order of access. This is true for disks, where the item requested probably just went by the read heads, and another rotation of the platter is required. Mechanical systems, in operation, tend to wear out due to mechanical causes. Electrical systems wear out as well, usually in a longer time.

A memory can be considered as a black-box with two functions, read and write. With the write function, we present the memory with two inputs: the data item, and an address. There is no output. The memory associates the data item with the address and remembers it. On the read function, we present the memory with the address, and expect to get back the data item previously associated with it.

Is there such a thing as totally non-volatile memory? Magnetic core was persistent when the power was turned off. It is unclear how long the data was/will be retained.

Other design choices in memory include volatility. The memory may forget after a period of time. That's not good. Although, depending on the timing, the data can be read out and written back just in time. One simple technology used in the early machines for entering data was the plug board. This was a xy grid of contact points, and one inserted little plugs to make connections.

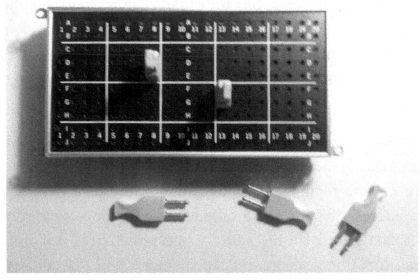

Plug board and jumper pins.

This was read-only memory, and nov-volatile. It was often used to enter constants. The plug boards could be large, on the order of 3 feet square.

18 pieces of 16-pin chips, 8-bit byte plus parity. The capacity of each chip is 64k bits.

Semiconductor memory was the game changer. It is small, dense, and needs little power. We can build both volatile and non-volatile memory. Early semiconductor memory was produced in small chips.

Power and heat generation

Mainframes were large consumers of electricity, and large generators of waste heat. The power supply for the IBM 7090, for example, used a large motor connected to standard 220 volt inputs, that was coupled to a 400 Hz, 3-phase generator. This made the alternating current easier to filter. Why not direct current? It is too hard to distribute, having large losses. (The author was working on such an IBM power supply as an undergrad when the bearing between the motor and alternator seized. The box flipped on its side before the breakers blew.)

As much power as they consumed, most went off as waste heat. Most mainframes needed a dedicated air conditioning plant, and sat on raised floors, that served not only for air flow, but for cabling between the boxes. Later mainframes, like the larger S/360's were water cooled.

Software

The compilation process involves taking your source code in COBOL or Fortran, and translating it to a language the computer understands, This is done...by a program – the compiler.

The step that translates your algorithm from an instantiation in a higher order language such as c into a language that the hardware understands is called compilation. Compilation involves both translation and optimization. Compilation can be done by hand, but it is certainly much easier with machine resources. It involves the translation of an algorithm or process, expressed in a user-friendly language, into a machine-readable format. It allows us to capture requirements and implement them in the unique hardware of the machine.

The compiler, itself a program, takes our code as input, and produces error messages – actually, it produces code for the target machine, usually in the form of assembly language. The higher order language statements, somewhat algebraic in form, translate into multiple assembly language statements. The compilation stage is followed by an assembly stage. Assembly language usually translates 1:1 into machine language.

The program is not necessarily compiled into one big lump of code – it may be modular. This allows code reuse. Modules may be stored in a library, and attached to the main program as required. Think of a square root routine as an example. The program that takes the output of the compiler, the various programs from the code library, and possibly some assembly language and puts it all together into one module is the linker.

The quality of the produced code reflects on the use of cpu resources, memory usage, performance (throughput), and quality.

The compiler can also do optimizations, both machine-independent, and machine or architecture dependent. We first have to understand what type of optimization (if any) is required: for space or time. We might require a small program, a fast program, or a small, fast program. We may optimize for energy use, or power consumption.

An operating system (OS) is a software program that manages computer hardware resources, and provides common services for execution of various application software. Without an operating system, a user cannot run an application program on their computer, unless the application program is self-booting.

For hardware functions such as input and output and memory allocation, the operating system acts as an intermediary between application programs and the computer hardware, although the application code is usually executed directly by the hardware and will frequently call the OS or be interrupted by it. Operating systems are found on almost any device that contains a computer. The OS functions are done by software, whether we call that software an OS or not.

An operating system manages computer resources, including memory, access to system resources, and time. In batch mode, on the mainframe, you essentially had all the machine resources to yourself during the run. Then, time sharing came along and you had to share. The operating systems enforced the sharing.

Predecessor Machines

This section will discuss the early pioneering computers. In many cases, only one was built. These pioneering machines drove the development of better technology for computation, storage, and communication. They defined the commercial product, the mainframe computer families. Initially, only governments could afford computers. Then it was big companies. Now, we all have them. They're everywhere.

Babbage's Analytical Engine

Computers do not need to be implemented in digital logic. They don't need to be electronic, or electrical at all. Charles Babbage's Differential Engine and Analytical Engine were large mechanical devices, operated by hand crank, capable of being upgraded to steam. Babbage started his work around 1837. There was a need for calculation assistance, both to speed up the process, and to control human error. Businesses and governments had a need for accurate mathematical tables and calculations related to tides and actuarial data.

The problem was not so much the calculations – that could be done by a room full of mathematicians. The problem was human error. After the results were obtained, they needed to be printer and disseminated.

You could type set the tables of numbers, but you couldn't proofread them. Babbage's machine included a printer and typesetter as output. If you programmed the problem correctly, you got hardcopy of your desired results.

Babbage didn't complete his project, for a number of reasons. He had to invent the technology to build the parts he needed to the required tolerances. There were no mechanical industry standards. He didn't get along with his Chief Mechanic, Whitworth, who left, and went on to standardize screw threads in the UK. Interchangeable parts – image that.

Although the mechanical industry was not capable of building Babbage's machine, it was way ahead of the electrical industry of the time. Babbage made the obvious choice to implement his architecture with mechanisms. He also chose decimal notation. Binary was known, but at the end, you had to translate to decimal. Thus, Babbage's design had 10 states, not 2. That was a big complication for machinery.

The Differential Engine was finally built over a period of 17 years, well after Babbages death, and is at the Science Museum in London. A second, privately-owned one is on loan at the Computer History Museum in Palo Alto, California. They are both operable.

The intricate mechanisms of the Differential Engine mesh together perfectly, and the computer is hand-cranked. This allows a skilled operator (and there are only several in the world) to "feel" the calculation, and avoid possible jams. A carry in a calculation is particularly awesome to watch.

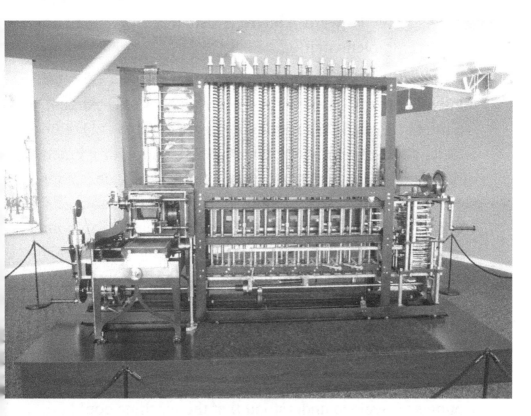

Second copy of Babbage's Difference Engine, built at Science Museum, Kensington (UK), and on exhibit at Computer History Museum, Palo Alto. Note the crank to the right. The printer is on the left. The tall columns are number accumulators.

Babbage left behind a treasure trove of documents and drawings. His son assembled some of the difference engine, and, more significantly, delivered a lecture about the machine at Harvard. The concepts directly influenced the design of Howard Aiken's ASSC machine, albeit an electronic implementation.

Babbage was written about extensively by his contemporaries. His biggest fan was Ada August, Countess Lovelace. She probably understood his machine and its applications better than he did. Victorian women didn't study mechanisms, and math, and "computer science." Well, Ada, while documenting Babbage's' work, taking care of several kids and households, in poor health, was tutored in math by de Morgan, and learned Calculus from Newton's book, in Latin. Interestingly, Boole was formulating the laws that would define logic, and de Morgan was coming up with the way to use binary logic to implement math. It just came together too late.

Countess Lovelace understood that the machine could not only crunch numbers, but could be used to compose and produce music. She writes about the machine programming itself. Since Babbage was already using input cards adapted from automated weaving, she understood that graphics could be produced from the machine, from mathematical functions. Babbage added a card punch to the design. They discussed what we would call Artificial Intelligence, in the sense of how much could the machine do on its own?

Both computer simulations and models of the Analytical Engine have been produced, but it still remains to make a working copy, from Babbage's diagrams. Of course, the machining technology has vastly improved since Babbage's time.

The Analytical Engine has been referred to as the Victorian Supercomputer. The Difference Engine, if finished, would have made a major impact on the British and world economy. The Analytical Engine would have been a game changer.

To date, the Analytical Engine has not been implemented. There is a project (www.Plan28.org) to do so. It was kicked off in 2010, and is being done in conjunction with the London Science Museum. The first product of the effort is the digitization of Babbage's notes and diagrams. These will be available to the public. After 100 years and more, the information will be available to a wide audience. The guy was just a little too early....what could have been?...

Colossus

Colossus was a British computer of World War-2, designed by Tommy Flowers to decrypt German messages encrypted by the Enigma machines. It employed some 1,500 vacuum tubes. It was able to decrypt intercepted coded messages in hours, as opposed to weeks. A total of ten machines were built, and later upgraded to a Mark-2 configuration. The first was working by December of 1943.

Colossus was the world's first electronic computer that was programmable. It performed cryptanalysis exclusively. It was operated at the Government Code and Cypher School at Bletchley Park, UK. It was programmed by plugs and switches.

After the war, most of the machines and documentation were destroyed in the interests of secrecy. Churchill directed it be "broken into pieces no larger than a man's hand."A functional replica was built in 2007, and may be seen at the National Museum of Computing, Bletchley Park.

ENIAC

This machine is considered to be the first digital general-purpose computer. It was re-programmable, not built for one specific task. Its initial job was to compute artillery firing tables for the Army's Ballistic Research Lab. The project kicked off in 1943. Before then, the firing tables had been calculated by rooms full of human *calculators,* sitting at desks with electromechanical adding machines. The idea of automating these routine tasks, and reducing errors, was very interesting. The work was done at the University of Pennsylvania's Moore School of Engineering. When the machine was revealed to the public in 1946, it had cost a half a million dollars. It operated at the Aberdeen Proving Grounds in Maryland from 1947 to 1955.

The ENIAC worked with 10-digit decimal numbers. It had 17,500 vacuum tubes (types 6SN7, 6L7, 6SJ7, 6AC7, 6L6, 6V6), more than 7,000 diodes, and 15,000 relays. There were some 5 million hand-soldered connections, a major source of problems. It took up some 1,800 square feet of floor space, weighed 30 tons, and used 150 kilowatts of power. The basic cycle time was 200 microseconds. It implemented the four basic math operations, plus square root.

The key to limiting tube failure was leaving the heaters switched on, not cycling on and off, and operating them at a reduced voltage. It was possible to configure the machine to handle double precision (20 digit) calculations.

ENIAC could accept input from an IBM card reader, and produce output to a card punch. The IBM 405 machine could accept the cards, and print their contents. Several tubes failed every day. Later, the failure rate was reduced to one tube every other day. It took 15 minutes or more to troubleshoot, locate, and replace the tube. By 1954, the machine had operated for almost 5 days continuously without a failure.

The ENIAC was used in calculations for the hydrogen bomb project, by John von Neumann. The data was one million punched cards. Programming the machine was tedious, and took days or weeks. Most of the programming was done by a team of women mathematicians. Their job title was *computer*. They configured the plug boards and switches. The machine was rewired between each job.

Only one ENIAC machine was built. Since ENIAC could not store its program (except as a physical configuration), it occurred to von Neumann that a program is just data of another sort, and could be treated as such. Most machines today use this *von Neumann architecture*. ENIAC was later modified in the field to include the stored program feature. In 1953, ENIAC received a 100 word memory upgrade, using core memory.

U.S. patent 3,120,606 for ENIAC, was granted in 1964, but voided in 1973, after re-examination of the Atanasoff-Berry Computer documentation of 1939.

Later, the circa November, 1971 4-bit Intel microchip, the 4004 processor, would have the same computer power as ENIAC. A functional FPGA version of the ENIAC was completed by University of Pennsylvania graduate students in 1995, and operated at 20MHz.

Parts of the ENIAC are on display at the Computer History Museum, the Smithsonian, University of Michigan, the Science Museum in London, Aberdeen Proving Grounds, US Military Academy at West Point, and at Perot systems in Texas.

EDVAC

EDVAC, the Electronic Discrete Variable Automatic Computer, came after ENIAC, and was a binary computer. Mauchly and Eckert suggested the design in August of 1944, and it was designed even before the ENIAC was operational. It incorporated many lessons-learned. It included, for example, a high speed serial memory. It used a thousand 44-bit words. There was a magnetic tape recorder, although this has sometimes been reported as a wire recorder. The control unit and console incorporated an oscilloscope. It implemented an internal timer, and the memory unit had two sets of 64 mercury delay lines, with eight words stored on each line. It could do a little over 1100 addition operations per second, and about 350 multiplys The memory access time was not deterministic, and depended on where the words were in the delay line.

The machine was comprised of some 6,000 vacuum tubes, and 12,000 diodes. It needed some 56 kilowatts of power. It used up almost 500 square feet of floor space, and weighted over 17,000 pounds. It had a crew of 30 people per shift, and operated around the clock. It was installed at the Army's Ballistics Research Laboratory at Aberdeen, Maryland in 1949. It began operations in 1951. there was a dispute over patent rights between the designers, Mauchly and Eckert, and the University of Pennsylvania, that lead the men to leave the University and form the Eckert-Mauchly Computer Corporation.

Punch card I/O was added in 1953, and it got a magnetic drum in 1954. Floating point capability was added in 1958. The machine was operational until 1961.

Whirlwind

Whirlwind was a different type of computer, developed by the MIT Servomechanisms Lab for the Navy. It was one of the first real-time systems, not designed for batch processing. It was implemented in vacuum tube technology. It became the model for the USAF's Semi

Automatic Ground System (SAGE). It was designed in 1947, and built from 1948 to 1951. It's purpose was to operate a flight simulator for aircraft. The first implementation was analog, but was not satisfactory. Influenced by ENIAC, a digital approach was designed.

The breakthrough was that the digital computer was driven by software, where the analog computer had to be reconfigured by hardware cables. Digital computers, up to this point were all run in batch mode, but Whirlwind dealt with changing inputs in a real-time environment.

Whirlwind had 16 math units, what we would today call ALU's, operating on 16-bit data. The instructions were contained in a control store, that fed the instructions to a diode decoding matrix.

When the machine was designed, the only viable storage was delay line or electrostatic tube. Read-only memory was implemented in toggle switches. Registers were implemented in vacuum tubes. Magnetic core memory was invented during the project, to overcome the limitations of the earlier storage methods. The team built a custom 1024 word core.

Special vacuum tubes were designed for long life. Interestingly, this involved removing silicon from the heater element.

The Whirlwind interfaced with radar equipment over phone lines, and tracked aircraft over New England. The Whirlwind can be seen in the Computer History Museum in Mountain View, California.

ASCC

The Automated Sequence Controlled Calculator, or Harvard Mark I, was the first digital calculator in the United States. It was built for Harvard University by IBM. It was a project designed by Howard Aiken, starting in 1937. It was a general purpose, electromechanical design It was influenced by Babbage's work, from a presentation given at Harvard by Babbage's son. It was employed by John von Neumann for work on the Manhattan project during World War 2. It was retired in 1959, and pieces still exist at Harvard.

Babbage would have appreciated the machine. It was constructed from switches, relays, rotating shafts, and clutches. It was 51 feet long x 8 feet x 2 feet, and weighed 5 tons. The main shaft was 50 feet long, driven by a 5 horsepower motor. It calculated to 18 decimal places.

Instructions came from 24 channel paper tape. There was no conditional branch instruction, so to execute the same code over and over, the paper tape was taped into a

...loop. The 24 bit instruction code contained an opcode, the source operand, and a destination.

Howard Aiken built more machines in house, based on experience with the Mark-I. Mark-III used vacuum tubes, but retained rotating magnetic drums for storage, and relays. Mark-IV was completely electronic.

IBM also learned a lot from the experience, and branched out from unit record equipment that simply read, punched, and printed cards. The first such machine that went into production, was IBM's 603, the Electronic Multiplier. This was followed by the 604 Electronic Calculating Punch, and the 650 Magnetic Drum calculator. The 702 model used magnetic tape. IBM was now heavily into computers.

SAGE

The IBM AN/FSQ-7 Combat Direction Center was a command and control system during the Cold War. It was designed for ground-based interception of incoming enemy bombers, and worked with the SAGE (Semi Automatic Ground Environment) defense network. It was possibly the largest computer system ever built, with 24 networked machines, each with dual redundant cpu's and weighing 250 tons. Each machine used 60,000 vacuum tubes with magnetic core memory, and required 3 megawatts of power. The core memory was organized as

71

32-bit words, with a parity bit. It had a 6-microsecond cycle time. The machines were capable of around 75,000 instructions per second. The design came from MIT's Lincoln Labs, with IBM Federal Systems providing the hardware and software. The Automatic Target and Battery Evaluation algorithm used radar data to calculate interception point for manned fighter aircraft and Bomarc missiles. The systems could essentially fly the manned system to the target aircraft, hands-off for the pilot.

The cpu had an accumulator register, a memory data register, a register for the least significant part of a multiplication, a program counter, and four index registers. The cpu clock was 166 KHz. The real time clock register used a 32 Hz clock. There were no interrupts implemented. Trigonometric functions (sine and cosine) were provided in look-up tables, with binary angles (256 division per 360 degrees).

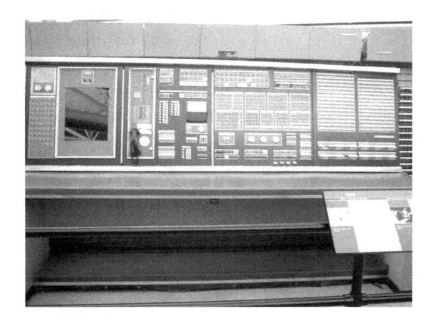

SAGE console at Computer History Museum, Palo Alto. Photo by author.

The SAGE system was a derivative of the earlier Whirlwind computer based systems, developed at MIT. The prototype was completed in 1955, and began running simulated Bomarc interceptions, and live interceptions of target drones flown from the Cape Canaveral station.

During the off-times, the Sage had been programmed to display dancing girls in grass skirts, according to a SAGE veteran. Video games are older than you might think. SAGE also had some computer music programs.

The architecture of the Whirlwind computer was precedent-setting, as it was the first real-time system. Construction was begun in 1948. It was a 16-bit design, with 2048 words of memory, using electrostatic technology, later changed to the recently developed magnetic cores memory.

The architecture of the SAGE computer systems used IBM standard peripherals such as card reader/punches, line printers, magnetic tape and drum memory. The computers were purpose-built to calculate intercepts, and influenced the design of the later Sabre airline reservation system.

The interesting problem with storing instructions on drum is that instructions could take longer to execute than the rotation time to the next storage slot. Thus, one had to carefully place the instructions on the drum, not necessarily in execution order. There were handy tables of instructions lengths to help you manually calculate this. Later, Loader programs could handle this themselves.

The SAGE systems was complex and costly, but never had to launch an intercept for real. In a sense, it helped preserve the peace during 25 years of turbulent times. The concept of linking the control centers with the radar sites over leased telephone lines influenced the later design of the ARPAnet, the predecessor of the Internet. The SAGE machine is preserved in the Computer History Museum.

Illiac IV

Illiac-IV was an ambitious project, a parallel supercomputer with 256 processors. Each processing element was capable of operating at 4 MIPS, on 64-bit data. It was implemented in ECL logic gates from Texas Instruments, which are fast, but power-hungry. There was one control unit for all 256 of the processing elements. Each processing element was connected to 4 of its neighboring units, and had 2k words of its own private memory. The goal for the machine, which was never achieved due to schedule issues, was 1 gigaflop of performance.

A Burroughs 6500 mainframe was used as a front end, and to handle input-output for Illiac. Burroughs disk drives of 80 megabyte capacity were used. There was also a laser optical storage system (cd/dvd) that could store up to 1 terabyte, but was a write-once design. It was programmed in a version of Parallel Fortran, or Parallel Algol.

The machine was based on a University of Illinois design by David Slotnick for massively parallel/vector architectures. It was funded by DARPA, but delivered to

NASA. It was, in the day, the fastest computer, some 13 times faster than its nearest competitor. It held that title until 1981.

Today, we classify the Illiac-IV as a SIMD machine – single instruction, multiple data. Illiac-IV certainly kicked off the Supercomputer era.

Illiac-IV was delivered to NASA-Ames in Mountain View, CA, and was connected to the Internet in 1975. It was 10 feet high by 8 feet deep, by 50 feet long. It used massive amounts of electricity, and was prone to overheating. Some Illiac modules can be seen at the Computer History Museum in California.

Manufacturers

In that time frame, late 1950's through 1970, the mainframe market was dominated by "IBM and the Seven Dwarfs." These were UNIVAC, NCR, Control Data, Honeywell, General Electric, RCA, and Burroughs. After two companies dropped out, the remaining were call "The Bunch": Burroughs, Univac, NCR, Control Data, and Honeywell.

Most of the machines were 32 bit, but Univac stuck with 36 bit words, using 6-bit bytes. The IBM dominance was due to their development of the System/360 series, from the legacy of their 704/7040 and 709/7090 machines. The follow-on machines to the S/360 architecture, the S/370, are still being produced. IBM supplied emulators that allowed you to run your 709 code on a new 7090, and your 7090 code on a S/360. That saved customers a lot of reprogramming hassle. It ran slower, but it ran. Certainly faster than on the old iron. It was not unheard of for a S/360 to run a 7090 emulator which emulated a 704.

IBM

IBM became to dominant force in mainframe computers, and is still to this day. We discuss some of the relevant products in this section.

The IBM 650 computer was based on a magnetic drum for storage. It consisted of three large cabinets, containing the type 650 operators console, the 655 power unit, and the type 533 punch card I/O device. It was a decimal machine, capable of holding 10,000 or 20,000 digits. It integrated nicely into organizations who were already using punch cards, and card sorters. It could handle 200 cards per minute, each holding up to 80 digits. The magnetic drum was in the Console Unit, as well as the actual processor, and a display console of switches and lights. Ten digit numbers could be added or subtracted, and 10 digit numbers could be multiplied, giving a 20 digit result. It could also divide a 20 digit number by a 10 digit number, giving a quotient and a remainder. Test instructions allowed for data-dependent

77

change in the flow of control. The hardware implemented a table-lookup function (TLU). A routine for calculating square roots could be implemented in 15 instructions, with 7 associated storage locations, and would take 0.252 seconds.

The drum rotation rate of 12,500 RPM set the basic operating speed of the machine. A word time was 0.96 milliseconds. The interesting challenge is putting your program on the drum was, that the time between storage locations was longer than the time to execute instructions. You could not load the program sequentially, but had to carefully space the instructions. A handy printed guide was available.

In the 650 architecture, a signed 10 digit number was a word. Data and intermediate results were stored on the rotating drum memory. An instruction consisted of a 2-digit op code, a 4 digit data address, and a 4 digit instruction address. The computer implemented a 20-bit accumulator register. The adder was bit-serial. Multiplication was accomplished by repeated addition, and division by repeated subtraction. There were 44 opcodes, including branch-on-non-zero, branch-on-minus, and branch-on-overflow. Data could be entered manually from the console switches.

Even though it was a decimal machine, it was possible to represent both a +zero and a -zero. Care had to be taken to ensure these tested equal. This is a problem in binary 1's complement representation of negative numbers.

There was no printer. If you wanted a printout, you took the card deck to another piece of equipment (an IBM 407 would work), which printed the information on the cards. Interestingly, if you hit the master power switch on the 650 during operation, the machine turned off immediately, and would not turn back on until a customer engineer from IBM reset it.

In 1959, IBM introduced the 1401, a variable word length decimal computer. It was meant to replace unit record equipment, which relied on paper card reading, punching, and sorting. This equipment, which had vastly simplified the US census in the 19th century, was a big improvement over large rooms full of clerks. Unit record equipment was based on mechanical systems. It was developed and commercialized by Herman Hollerith. Using this equipment, the 1890 census was finished "ahead of schedule and under budget." How often does that happen?

In 1884, Hollerith filed for a patent on the "Art of Compiling Statistics," which was granted in 1889 as U. S. Patent 395,782.

The 1401 could be rented from IBM, starting at $2,500 per month. They got 5,200 orders in the first 5 weeks. There were more than 10,000 units operating in industry by the mid 1960's, representing half of the computers in use in the world. The 1401 could operate as a stand-alone card-based batch processing system, and could also be used as a peripheral controller for larger machines such as the IBM 7090, which was faster at math. When the author was an incoming freshman at Carnegie Tech in Pittsburgh, student registration was handled by a 1401. The 1401 were sold until 1971. It was considered a second generation machine.

When the newer S/360 models came out, many customers wanted to avoid re-programming. IBM addressed this by providing a 1401 emulation model for some of the S/360 models, including the model 30. Custom 1401 models were targeted to banking.

The 1401 was a 6-bit machine. Punched cards provided the input. The memory ranged from 1.4k words to 16k words. An opcode was 1 character. The machine was implemented in diode-transistor logic (DTL) on SMS, or Standard Modular System cards. These were the equivalent of one of the later 7400-series TTL chips, a few logic gates, or a pair of flip-flops. The memory was magnetic core, with parity. Expansion memory of 16 k (yes, k) was in a second box of about 2 feet by 2 feet by 3 feet. The machine cycle time was 11.5 microseconds.

The 1401 got started when the LOAD button on the associated 1402 card punch/reader was pressed. This was the bootstrap process. A card was read into memory locations 1-80 (there are 80 columns on a card, each holding one character). Execution started at location 1. A lot of useful programs only needed one card. There was even a one card "Hello, World" program to the line printer. The cards following the program card or cards would contain the data.

There was a lot of software support for the 1401. This included an assembler, Autocoder, an advanced assembler, Cobol, Fortran-II, Fortran-IV, RPG (report program generator) and others. Many of these required multiple IBM 729 7-track tape drives to be attached to the system.

One "hack"that was popular with late night 1401 programmers was the music program, using a transistor radio sitting on the cabinet, with music produced by combining various operations.

The 1401 used a variety of peripherals. There were several card reader/punches, several printers, several tape drives, later, several disk drives, and a check processing peripheral. Paper tape I/O was also supported. The

Computer History Museum has 2 operational 1401 systems.

The IBM 701 was the first large scale electronic computer manufactured in quantity in 1951. It was a scientific machine. It used Williams tubes for memory.

The circa 1954 IBM 704 has the distinction of being the first mass-produced computer to implement floating point hardware. It used vacuum tubes for the logic function, but core for memory. It introduced 15-bit index registers for address modification, and was a 36-bit architecture. It was intended for the scientific market, and achieved 12,000 floating point adds per second. A total of 140 units were sold. The 704 introduced the programming languages Fortran and LISP. It was also the platform for the first real computer music program. A 704 at Bell Labs was used to synthesize human speech in 1962.

Peripherals for the 704 included the 711 Card Reader, 721 Card Punch, the 716 line printer, the 727 Magnetic Tape Unit (5 million 6-bit characters) with the 753 Tape controller, the 733 Drum memory, and the 737 Core memory (4096 36-bit words). The 740 Cathode Ray Tube output recorder (CRT) was also available for an extra cost. As with most machines of the era, data could be entered by switches on the operator console.

The 709 was an improved 704 that came out in 1958. It had some new instructions, could do overlapped I/O, and indirect addressing was implemented. A hardware emulator was available to allow the execution of legacy 704 code. Fortran came out for the 709. The 709 introduced IBM's I/O channel architecture, using the model 766 Data synchronizer. Three units could be used, each controlling up to 20 tape drives. These essentially offloaded I/O from the main cpu. The upgraded 738 Magnetic Core Storage substituted transistor-based sense amps for earlier tube -based units.

The 7030 Stretch was an IBM supercomputer that was delivered in 1961. It was seven times faster than the 7090. It used transistor technology. The first unit went to Los Alamos National Laboratory in 1961, with the second unit going to NSA at Fort Meade, MD, in 1962. This latter unit was a customized version, called the 7950. A total of 9 were delivered. The initial unit price was $13,500,000, but that was nearly halved when the machine failed to achieve it's projected performance of 100 times that of the IBM 704. The actual performance was about 30 times that of the 704. It has the distinction of being the fastest computer in the world from 1961 to 1964. It provided many design features to the later S/360 series. It was implemented with 170,000 transistors.

Variable length fixed point numbers were implemented in decimal or binary. They were either unsigned, or sign-magnitude format. Floating point was also supported. Alpha and special characters were implemented in 8 bits. Instructions took one or two 32-bit words. The 32 registers were mapped into the lower end of the memory address. Memory was implemented in 16k banks, and went to 256k 64-bit words. The core memory was immersed in oil to maintain a consistent temperature, and timing. Gene Amdahl was instrumental in the Stretch design.

The Stretch project developed the SMS or Standard Modular System TTL modules, that were used in later IBM machines. It introduced such key concepts as memory protection, the 8-bit byte, generalized interrupts, multiprogramming, and more. Parts of two 7030's can be seen at the Computer History Museum in California.

The IBM 7040 came out in 1963. It was a 36-bit machine. The 7044 was a faster version of the 7040. Both machines could do double precision floating point calculations. A 7040 could serve as an I/O processor for a 7090 in a tightly coupled multiprocessor configuration. This line was introduced after the 7090, as a lower cost alternative. The machines used peripherals from the previous 1401 series. Integers were represented in sign-magnitude format. Single precision floating point had a

27 bit magnitude, with a 8-bit exponent. The batch operating system was called IBSYS.

The 7090 was a transistor-based machine, appearing in 1959. It retained the 36 bit word, using the 7302 Core memory developed on the Stretch project. The 7090 was some six times faster than the earlier 709. Dual IBM 7090's were the basis of the first commercial airline reservation system, American Airlines' Sabre, in 1958. In addition, the 7090's were used as part of the Sylvania AN/FSQ-28 Missile Impart Predictor, an integral part of the BMEWS (Ballistic missile early warning system), and the Radar Central computer in this Cold War project.

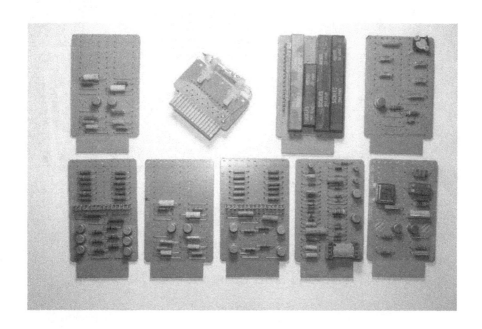

7090/94 circuit cards with discrete components

The 7090 introduced IBM's data channel architecture, where I/O was off-loaded from the main processor. Up to 8 channels could be used, with support for up to ten model 729 tape drives per channel. An I/O channel had its own instructions, which were passed over from the main cpu. These were effectively a channel program, allowing I/O to proceed without further processor intervention. Channel controllers could also host paper tape, card equipment, printers, and disks as well.

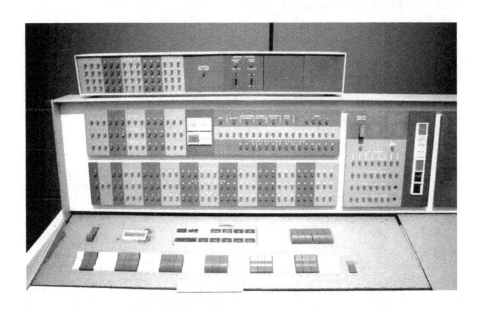

7094 Console (I sold mine on ebay)

A faster solution was to re-purpose a 1401 as an I/O controller in a 709x system. Multiple 1401's could be used, depending on the volume of I/O.

The 7094 was an advanced version, introduced in 1962. It expanded the index register's to seven, from three. On it's console was a new added box to display the contents of the four new index registers. The '94 added double precision floating point support. These were a 54-bit magnitude with the 8-bit exponent. In 1964, a 7094 Mod-II was introduced with twice the speed of its predecessor. Part of the performance gain was due to an instruction pipeline architecture.

7090's and 7094 supported NASA's Mercury and Gemini manned flights. The Apollo missions used the newer S/360 machines.

The batch operating system for the 7090 was also called IBSYS, but was different from the 7040 version. It was based on Fortran. It's job was to read the special control cards in the user's deck (the deck consisted of control cards, program cards, and data cards.) A control card was distinguished by a "$" in column 1. Most of the operating system was resident on tape, and specific routine required by the program were read into memory as needed.

The IBM System/360 architecture defined a family of 32-bit machine's that would span the spectrum of commercial and scientific needs. Interestingly, IBM said "...the measurement of the system would not be solely in events per microsecond, but more important, in answers per dollar per month." Customers were becoming more cost sensitive, and the big machines were no longer a novelty, but a commodity. The S/360 generally used card input, printer output, tape, disk, and drum storage. There was a family of processors, from the low end model 20 through the supercomputer class model 95. There were eventually fourteen models eventually, including some custom models to support the U. S. Space Program and the lunar landings. They shared the same set of peripheral units, channel controllers, mass storage, and I/O. The operating system 0S/360 was the same across platforms.

The chief architect of the S/360 was Gene Amdahl, and it was managed by Fred Brooks, author of "The Mythical Man-Month," the ultimate lessons-learned.

Although the family architecture was the same, the implementations differed. This was not visible to the user. To keep things in the family, IBM had long offered backward compatibility for its new computers, to protect the customer's investment in software development. The S/360 model 30 could emulate a 1401, and a model 65 could pretend to be a 7094. This required an emulation program, supplied by IBM. It was said a S/360 could emulate a 7090 emulating a 1401, which gave about the same performance as the original 1401 hardware.

Mainframe I/O was offloaded in the S/360 architecture to Communication channels, essentially, a computer who job it was to interface with storage and devices and printers. The Channel offloaded these asynchronous tasks from the main computer part, allowing it to function more efficiently on big calculations. Peripherals of the period included card readers, line printers, magnetic tape drives, data storage drums, and later, disks. Memory in the units was magnetic core. The circuitry was transistor based, a big improvement on the previous generation's vacuum tubes. Integrated circuits would come later.

The S/360 architecture drove a series of industry standards. The 8-bit byte, and the EBCDIC character set, memory that was addressable by byte, floating point (which evolved into the IEEE 754 standard), and 9 track tapes. No more 7-track.

IBM 9-track tape with the author's homework assignments..

The S/360 architecture was big-endian, meaning the most significant bit or byte was at the lowest address of a word. The architecture had sixteen 32-bit general purpose registers. A 64-bit program status word (PSW) was provided. Interrupts were maskable, except for a critical few. Memory was organized into 8-bit bytes, with 24 bit addressing.

(That is sitting on my desk, as I type.)

Front panel of the S/360 Multiplexer Unit. These were always painted "IBM Blue"

You got a S/360 mainframe going after power-on by a bootstrap processed called IPL, or Initial Program Load. At the console, you select a three hex digit address of the device you wanted to boot from. You push the LOAD button. The boot program (24 bytes) from the selected device (usually a disk) is read into memory, starting at address zero. These are treated as channel command words, which execute channel (or, I/O) commands to read in the rest of the program. The PSW is loaded. It contains the initial address to start execution from. A tape or even a card reader can be used as the boot device. On a disk, the channel command causes the selected device to seek to cylinder 0000h, head 0000h for record 01h. A similar process was used later to boot the IBM pc.

IBM S/360

The System needed more than a cpu, and IBM had a full line of input/output and storage peripherals. These included both typewriter and video based display units, card I/O, printers, optical character readers, communications units, and disk, Datacell, drum, and tape storage.

The IBM 2321 Data Cell was a circa-1964 secondary storage device faster than tape, not as fast as disk. The storage capacity of the refrigerator-sized device was 400 Megabytes. Data were stored on removable strips of magnetic material, arranged in bins in a drum configuration.

The early 1960's design was from Alan Shugart, later involved in the disk business. Each data cell unit had 10 cartridges, and each cartridge held 200 magnetic cards. These were 3"x15". The total capacity of the unit was 40 megabytes. Average access time for a card was about 0.5 seconds. The Datacell had problems with physically access the cars and returning them to the proper cartridge.

When data was accessed, the assembly rotated to the correct bin, and the correct magnetic strip was removed and read. This was accomplished by a mechanism using Mobil DTE hydraulic fluid at 1,500 psi. Where are we going with this? Stay with me here.

Each magnetic strip held about 200k bytes. If one were to write a program to multiply two matrices, one of which was on a particular strip, and the other was on a strip 180 degrees away, a large of amount of time would be consumed by thrashing, and the drum rotated back and forth to access the next data item. The hydraulic system kept this going until the bearings burned out. Not that I would have tried this.

This is an example of making your data cache size commensurate with your data structure. This resulting in what is called data thrashing.. The matrix operation could overheat the data cell drive assembly, and cause the bearing to fail.

IBM Data Cell drive

Data Cell segment in transport container.

Most installations used the 1052 Printer-Keyboard as a console device. This unit was similar to a Selectric typewriter. The 2250 display unit had a 21 inch CRT tube, and could be used as the operators console. It displayed alphanumeric data, or vectored video. The associated 2840 display control could handle multiple tubes. The controller had a character generator, and 8k bytes of core. The display could be equipped with a light pen. A film recorder was also supported.

Magnetic tape was a very popular media, because a tape drive could support mounting and unmounting many,

many tapes. These could be stored in archives, and were somewhat permanent. The vinyl tape did need to be spooled every few years or so, otherwise it stuck to itself on the reel. Tape storage was, unfortunately, serial access. You needed to read down the tape to get to where the data you wanted was stored. Tape generally had a directory at the front, with a a list of files names and where the data was, in terms of tape sectors. The IBM S/360 used the 2400 series tapes. This came in single or double drives. Drives were available in three speed ratings, 30, 60, and 90000 bytes per second. Each tape controller handled 8 drives. The drives were the size of refrigerators. The tape was ½ inch wide, 9 track. When you read to the end of the reel, the rewind time was several minutes. The tape handling in the drives was fairly good, and tapes were not damaged very often. If they broke, they could be spliced, and copied to another reel. The first part of the tape was most frequently used, and could wear out, producing errors. This was countered by copying the data, cutting off and discarding the first few feet of tape, and re-using the rest. Older 7-track tape could be read as an option. The drives implemented error detection and correction. With these drives, you did not need to carefully thread the tape over the drive wheels and read/write heads. The drives had an autoload feature. Drives could also read tape backward, eliminating the need for frequent rewinding.

A higher speed, higher density was offered with the 1"
hypertapes. These could read at more than 100 inches per
second (recording density was 1500 or 3000 bytes per
inch). The Hypertapes were enclosed in cartridges, to
minimize handling and contamination. Up to 16 drives
could be handled by a controller.

You could also get the 2671 paper tape reader for your
S/360 installation, working on 5-, 6-, 7-, or 8-channel
paper tape at 1000 characters per second. It was best to
update all your old paper-tape based data to magnetic
media as soon as possible. Paper tape could, however, be
fixed with adhesive tape.

The 2302 disk storage unit supported one or two disk
modules (depending on model). Each module had a little
more than 112 megabytes. Four modules could be
connected to a 2841 storage controller. The disk units
supported random access. The storage modules could
also be removed and replaced, like tape. The fashionable
user did not carry around huge decks of cards, or multiple
tapes, but would be seen with a personal disk cartridge.
The 2311, washing machine-sized, used the IBM 1316
disk packs. Each disk pack contained six platters. There
were 10 record-able surfaces, the top and bottom outside
surfaces not being used. The established size was a 14
inch diameter. The 2311 stored 7.25 megabytes on the
model 1316 disk pack. The data transfer rate was over

150 kbytes per second. The pack weighed ten pounds. The 2314 unit increased the capacity to 29 megabytes.

The IBM 1311 Disk Storage Unit held 2 million characters in a cabinet the size of a washing machine. It used the removable IBM 1316 disk pack. This accessory weighed ten pounds The device was introduced in 1962, and used well into the 1970's.

The IBM 2301 Drum storage unit was a random access device of four megabytes capacity. It could transfer data faster than 1 megabyte per second. Data were access in parallel for 4 tracks at at a time, out of 800 total tracks. Four drums could be attached to a storage controller. The unit was refrigerator-sized.

To get that data into the computer, the venerable 1401 card reader was used. This was part of the original 1401 computer equipment. The model N1, used with S/360, could read 1,000 cards per minute, and punch cards at 250 per minute. Another legacy unit was the 1403 printer. It could do 1,000 lines of type per minute. It was a chain printer, with the characters on a continuous metal chain, spinning at high speed. Different character sets could be supplied as different chains. Ten characters per inch was supported, with either 6 or 8 lines per inch. It was very impressive when the high speed chain broke.

Other specialty peripherals were also available. These included the 1412 and 1419 Magnetic Character reader, used to read checks, and the 1418 and 1428 optical character readers. The 1231 could read marks made by lead pencils in fixed boxes, and your SAT's were probably scored this way.

The System/360 was not limited to batch jobs. It could communicate with remote terminals through the 2701 data adapter unit. These allowed communications with the 1050 and 1060 data communication systems over the phone system (via a Dataset 103A), over a leased line, or via Western Union's network. Western Union was the fastest at 1280 bps. A later model supported 600 bps over leased, four-wire circuits. Teletypes could be interfaced at 100 bps.

The communications adapter also provided generic synchronous serial and parallel communications, and could read 48 switch closures. Automated data collection stations could be located remotely, and feed their data back to the S/360. The 1030 and 1050 supported remote data collection. A special system, the 1060, was used to connect a bank teller station tot the machine. The 1070 was for process control, with support for 300 I/O lines

The S/360 series used the IBM channel architecture for I/O. This offloaded the handling of I/O from the main cpu, to a smart controller. There were two types of channels, the selector, and the multiplexer. The 2860 was the selector channel controller, and the 2870 was used for the multiplexed channels. In addition, the 2880 was a block multiplexer

Author's Bell 103A data set

The channel has direct access to the memory, so it can transfer data to and from the main memory via DMA. It can also get the cpu's attention with an interrupt. Between the channel and the I/O device, data were transferred byte-at-a-time.

The 2860 selector channel came with 1, 2, or 3 channels. Data transfer speeds of 1.3 megabytes per second were supported. The channel controllers provided buffering. Up to eight I/O devices could be attached. Selector channels operated in burst mode.

The 2870 multiplexer channel addressed medium and low speed devices. Up to 192 subchannels supported up to 192 devices. A channel command to the channel controller from the cpu consisted of an 8-bit command code, a 24-bit address, a 5 bit flag, and an unsigned half-word (16 bits) count. The concept of channel I/O carried over into microprocessors, as Intel developed the 8089, a communications co-processor for the 8086 cpu.

JCL, or Job Control Language, was a scripting language to define a batch program for the S/360. The intricacies of JCL syntax was as easy as Latin or Classical Greek. The unit of work on the mainframe was a job. Jobs might contain one or more programs, and their associated data. The first card in the deck was the Job card, containing information on the user and the job, and its priority. Procedures could be predefined in JCL, and included as necessary. Besides the job card, there were one or more EXEC cards, defining the program to be run, and Data Description (DD) cards, identifying associated data files. Each JCL statement had a rigid structure of 5 fields. JCL statements were conditionally executable, based on program outputs.

The low end model S/360-30 shipped in mid-1965, as a scientific or commercial machine, with up to 64k bytes of memory. Model 44 supported real time computing and process control. The models 65 and 67 came in dual cpu-versions.

The Model 67 was unique in supporting dynamic address translation (ie, memory management for virtual memory). These had a large address translation unit, which allowed a special Operating System version for timesharing, TSS/360. This software was not successful, and was replaced by CP-67, which is still used on IBM Mainframes today.

The Model 75 was an outgrowth of IBM's continuing engineering development effort to enhance the capabilities of the original System/360 offerings. Its main memory operated at 750 nanoseconds and was available in three sizes up to 1,048,576 characters of information. The memory was interleaved up to four ways to obtain increased performance.

The Model 75 superseded the original Model 70 of the System/360 family, which had been announced a year earlier. Manufactured at IBM's plant in Kingston, N.Y., the Model 75 had a monthly rental range of $50,000 to $80,000, and a purchase price range from $2.2 million to $3.5 million. Deliveries began during the fourth quarter of 1965.

The Real Time computer complex at Mission Control at JSC was based on five S/360 model 75 IBM mainframes.

The previous Gemini Missions had been supported by up to five of the IBM 7094-II computers. The Control Center in Houston got the first S/360 shipped by IBM. The operating system OS/360 was not well suited to real time operations, being designed for batch processing. IBM introduced a real-time version, RTOS/360, with better real time response.

The Model 75 was near the top of the System/360 family in terms of size and performance. In the System/360, an 8-bit byte was standardized, and memory was byte addressable. Words were 32-bits in size, in big-endian format. CPU's were microcoded, and floating point operations were supported. Twenty-four bit addressing was supported, as were prioritized interrupts, crucial for real-time operation.

The Model 91 implemented out-of-order instruction execution, but dumped the decimal instruction set for commercial applications. It came out in November of 1962, with up to 4 megabytes of memory. The Model 95 was special order, available by 1968. Performance was more than 3.5 MIPS, with up to 5 megabytes of storage. Everything about a '91 was big.

S/360-91 console.

The S/360 architecture evolved into the S/370 architecture by 1970, and was the basis for the AP-101 flight computers used on the Space Shuttle. Special radiation hard, mil-spec S/360's fly on USAF aircraft.

The System S/370 models, successor to the S/360, included virtual memory support. The VM/370 operating system implemented virtual machines. The further evolution of the architecture was System z. It is code compatible, back 50 years. You could probable still run the 1401 emulator.

The IBM "Mainframe-on-a-chip" was the Micro/370, of 1980 vintage. This was originally envisioned as a desktop

S/360. The S/370 instruction set was implemented on a 32-bit Motorola 68000 chip, using microcode. A customized Intel 8087 floating point coprocessor was also used. These occupied one of three cards added to the pc. Another was a memory card, and the third implemented a model 3277 terminal. The set of cards was called the XT/370. There was also a project in IBM to develop a 370 microprocessor in 1985. It was a S/370 cpu, implemented in a microcoded 68000, and used the 68000 bus, not a S/370.

S/370 decedents are hard at work today in big data centers, managing your data, bank accounts, and travel plans. The Smithsonian has a S/360-65, and the Computer History Museum has a Model 30. A model 91 is preserved at the IBM Museum in Germany.

Burroughs

Burroughs Corporation's origins go back to 1886, as the American Arithmometer Company. They produced mechanical adding machines, typewriters, and later, computers. It was at one time the largest adding machine company in America. The company also produced a line of check processing machines for banks. Burroughs merged 100 years later with Sperry to become Univac.

The entry point into computers was Burroughs' purchase of ElectroData Corp of Pasadena, CA, in 1956. Soon, the B205, a tube-based computer, was brought to market.

Burroughs produced a full line of peripheral products for its computers, including printers, tape drives, disks, printer paper, and ribbons. Burroughs had the fastest card readers available, reaching 1000 cards per minute. (each card would contain 1 source line of code). The B2500 was oriented to business users, and used BCD-encoded decimal numbers. They were programmed in Cobol.

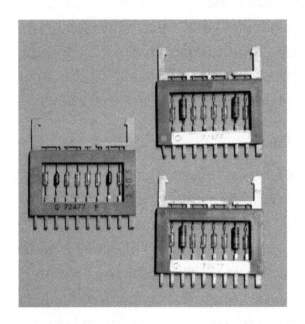

Discrete component modules from Burroughs.

In 1961, Burroughs introduced the B5000, followed by the B5500. The 5000 had drum memory, where the newer 5500 used disk. The 5700 supported multiple cpu's. The 6700 and 7700 could have up to seven cpu's. This line continued through the 7000 series in the 1970's. These were 48-bit stack machines, running Algol-60. The operating system was the Master Control Program, MCP.

The Atlas missile guidance system was based on a ground based, Burroughs computer. The Atlas missile was the result of the von Neumann ICBM Committee. Atlas A, B, C, and D had no onboard computers and used ground-based guidance Atlas was the first intercontinental ballistic missile deployed by the United States.

The AN/GSQ-33, Burroughs SM-65 was the ground-based missile guidance computer for the early Atlas series of rockets. Eventually 17 units were delivered. The ones at the Eastern Test Range (Cape Canaveral) and Western Test Range (Vandenberg AFB) were used for range safety until 1978. The reliability specification was 0.96, but the machine achieved an operational reliability of 0.998. There were no errors during flights. One machine operated 24 hours per day continuously for 17 months without a critical failure.

The data word size was 28 bits, and the instruction word was 18 bits. It was a binary machine, with 38 instructions. Clock speed was just above 200 Khz. An ADD operation took 47 microseconds, and a multiply took 532 microseconds.

Memory held 1536 instructions, core had room for 256 data items. Some constants could be set by switches. The machine required 208 volt power, 60 cycle, 3 phase, 20 kva from a motor-generator set. Although the cpu used transistor technology, the terminal equipment used tubes. The system included a paper tape reader, paper tape punch, and a plotter. As a real-time control computer, the machine received missile position and velocity data from radar, and produced steering commands for transmission to the vehicle.

Development of the computer started in 1955. It was a break in tradition from the tube-type computers that were common – it was transistorized. There were three models, developed incrementally. At the time that Burroughs was contracted for the computer, there was no Atlas missile in existence. After the computer was delivered, it was termed the AN/GSQ-33, Digital Computing System. There was some thought of making a truck-mounted "portable" system, but this was never developed.

The machine was implemented with direct-coupled transistor logic. The main problem was the connection between cabinets. If a cable was disconnected while powered, the driver transistor would burn out. This was encountered at the Smithsonian by the author after a large number of failures were noted during debugging of the unit.

Inter-cabinet connector.

Later, Burroughs teamed up with the University of Illinois to develop the Illiac-IV Supercomputer. Burroughs maintained a Defense and Space Computer Group in Paoli, PA. They spun off from this effort the 48-bit D825, which was a real-time machine, addressing airline reservations. TWA got one in 1965, although the machine did not work out.

Control Data Corp

Control Data was best known for its supercomputers, in the 1960's. Chief Designer Seymour Cray continually produced the fastest machines in the world while working for CDC. In the 1970's, he left to form his own company, Cray Research. CDC left the computer field in the 1980's.

The origins of CDC date from World War two, and a Navy code breaking team. To keep the unique team together, a new company, Engineering Research Associates was formed. One project was an early stored program commercial computer, the ERA-1103. ERA was later sold to Remington Rand., and the ERA-1103 became the Univac 1103, designed by Cray in 1953. It used 36 Williams tubes of 1024 bytes capacity each for memory, those being replaced in the 1103A by magnetic core. Magnetic drum units were used for secondary storage. Word size was 36 bits. It went in direct competition to IBM's 701. The 1104 was a follow-on to support the Bomarc missile program. Control Data, with Cray in the driver's seat, continued their interest in drum memory. The CDC 1604, a 48 bit machine, was delivered to the Navy in 1959. CDC produced tape drives as well as card readers, punches, and printers.

The big machine was the CDC6600. Cray was using the fast silicon transistors from Fairchild Semiconductor. Introduced in 1964, it blew away the competition by being ten times faster than anything else on the market. More than 100 units were sold. The computer had ten external I/O processors, to offload these tasks from the main cpu.

CDC 6600

The 7600 had a hardware speed of four times that of the 6600, and make extensive use of pipelining the instruction execution. It had, unfortunately, a different operating system than its predecessor. It also had reliability issues. In spite of this, about 30 were delivered.

The follow-on 8600 had four of the 7600's in one box. It had maintenance and thermal issues, and Cray redesigned it as the CDC Star-100. This was a vector processor, a SIMD architecture. It was after this that Cray left to form his own company. CDC finally left the computer industry by 1999, with pieces of the company going to British Telecomm.

The CDC-924A was a transistor-based mainframe computer. This was a 24-bit version of the 48-bit CDC 1604. They used magnetic core memory for storage. The 1600 series was used as the guidance computer (ground-based) for the Minuteman missile. You can see a CDC-

924 in the first Terminator movie, where it runs the machinery in a factory.

General Electric

A persistent story is that GE got into the computer business in the 1950's, because they were the second largest users of computers in the world, besides the U. S. Government. The company had also been the first owner of a computer, outside the government, and became the largest user of IBM mainframes. They produced a series of computers that found application in real time process control and industrial automation, timesharing, and for message switching and front end processing for larger computers. GE partnered with MIT and Bell Labs to develop the Multics operating systems for the GE645 model. Multics was arguably the predecessor to Bell Labs' Unix.

The 645 was a 36-bit machine, with channel controllers to offload I/O operations from the main CPU. The 645 model supported floating point operations, and virtual addressing of memory. It was constructed with discrete TTL chips. Core was used for memory. The earlier 635 model could contain 4 cpu's, a master and three slaves.

The GE computing division was sold to Honeywell in 1970. The GE-600 series was renamed the Honeywell 6000 series. Honeywell extended the instruction set with new instructions to support business applications written in Cobol.

Honeywell

Honeywell's introduction to the computer business was a join venture with Raytheon, called Datamatic Corporation. That later became Honeywell Information Systems. When Honeywell purchased Computer Control Corporation, it became the Computer Control Division.

Honeywell developed a competitor to the IBM 1401, which was known as the Honeywell 200. In 1970, Honeywell acquired the computer systems division of GE. In 1989, Honeywell exited the computer business, selling its computer division to Groupe Bull.

NCR

John H. Patterson founded the National Cash Register Company, maker of the first mechanical cash registers, in 1884. Focusing mostly on business machines in the early years, NCR acquired Computer Research Corporation (CRC), of Hawthorne, CA in 1952. This brought in a company that produced a line of digital computers with applications in aviation. This lead to an electronic banking machine. NCR partnered with GE to produce a transistor computer, the NCR 304, in 1957. In 1962, the NCR 315 Data Processing System, a 12-bit machine was released. The basic unit of memory was called a slab or syllable, 12 bits plus parity. Forty kilobits of memory took up 4 refrigerator-sized cabinets. The main cpu was three cabinets in size, and the console included an IBM Selectric typewriter.

The model 315-100 was similar, but the IBM Selectric was replaced by a teletype printer/keyboard. This model also introduced Automatic Recovery Option. The Model 315-RMC used thin film magnetic memory

The 315-RMC also supported floating point operations. These machines were programmed in Assembly and Cobol. Peripherals included a 600 line per minute printer, various magnetic drives, paper tape reader and punches, card reader and punch, drum memory, and optical character readers, mainly used for check processing.

NCR had the CRAM (Card Random Access Method) system in 1962. These used 3" x 14" cards. They supported 256 and 512 cards, providing up to 11 megabytes of storage. If you could fit 16 of the CRAM cabinets in a room, you could have 176 megabytes of storage. As with other mechanical units, card handling was a problem.

In 1991, NCR was acquired by AT&T and NCR purchased Teradata Corporation, acquiring its advanced and unique commercial parallel processing technology.

In 1994, the NCR name was changed to AT&T Global Information Solutions (GIS).

RCA

RCA was set up after World War-I by the General Electric Corporation. It went on to produce home appliances, vinyl record technology, personal radio receivers, televisions, vacuum tubes; and assorted electronics for consumer and government use.

RCA got into the computer business in the 1960s. Their Spectra 70 series were hardware compatible with IBM's S/360, but not software compatible. They were early innovators in timesharing and virtual memory machines. RCA exited the computer business in 1971.

The circa-1961 RCA-110 Computer Mainframe served as the checkout and launch control computer for the Apollo Saturn Vehicle. One was located in each of the four firing rooms in the Launch control Complex. There was another underground at each launch pad, and one on each of the Mobile Launch Platforms. The test software was developed at the Astrionics Lab at MSFC with support from the launch support team in Florida. The RCA-110A models had increased memory over the earlier 110 model. The computer automated the entire preflight checkout process. The master computer in the blockhouse and the slave computer at the launch pad were connected by a coaxial cable. The launch pad computer interfaced with the vehicle's computer in the Instrument Unit through an umbilical.

The RCA-110 was a 24-bit fixed-point process control machine. It was implemented in solid-state electronics, with a clock speed of 936 KHz, and had 72 instructions. It supported four levels of priority interrupts, and had accumulators and index registers. There were also eight Input-Output registers. The add or subtract operation took 57 microseconds, a multiply took 728 microseconds, and a divide, 868 microseconds.

Memory consisted of 256 to 4096 words of core memory, later expanded. Secondary storage was provided by a magnetic drum assembly, rotating at 3,600 rpm, and providing 8.3 millisecond access to data. The drum held up to 51,200 words. Data were transferred to the computer at a 200 kilohertz rate. The computer unit was 82" x 34" x 105" in size, and required 5,000 watts of power at 220 volts.

The RCA 301 Computer was a mainframe targeted to business users. It was a solid state design, with magnetic cores. It supported up to 40 kbytes of memory, and hosted magnetic tape drive, paper tape, punched cards, or RCA's RACE magnetic storage unit. The storage cards were 4" x 18" and the unit operated similarly to the IBM datacell. They had the nasty habit of ejecting bent or damaged cards at high speed from the unit, endangering the lives of computer operators in the area.

The Spectra 70 series was a family of computers, upwardly compatible from the base model. Memory was core based, and ranged from 4k bytes, to ½ megabyte. The peripherals were compatible across the computer line. The smaller units could serve as I/O processors for the larger models. Card readers, printers, paper tape, mag tape, magnetic drum and disk, and an optical character reader were available. Multiprocessors were supported. A communications multiplexer allowed the support of up to 256 dedicated lines, for time sharing applications. The Spectra series 70/45 started the third generation of mainframes, using integrated circuit technology. RCA exited the computer business in 1971. Sperry Rand took over RCA's computer business.

Univac

Univac, or Universal Automatic Computer, was developed by the ENIAC team, Eckert and Mauchly, as a commercial product. It was the second commercial computer made in the US. The first machine was delivered to the US Census Bureau in 1951. The fifth machine, which belonged to the Atomic Energy

Commission, corrected predicted the results of the 1952 Presidential Election (Eisenhower won) from early data.

The Command, Communication, and Telemetry System (CCATS) for the Apollo Missions used three Univac 494 computers. These were 30-bit machines with 131K to 262K of core memory. Up to 24 I/O channels were available and the system was usually shipped with UNIVAC magnetic drum storage. The basic operating system was OMEGA.

The AN/USQ-20 was the Naval Tactical Data system. Seventeen were delivered in 1961. A more generic version was the Univac 1206. Another variant was named the G-40, and replaced the previous 1104 for supporting the Bomarc missile development. This refrigerator-sized machine used 30-bit words, and had 32k of core.

The Univac 1 weighed close to 15 tons, needed 400 square feet of floor space, and used 125 KW of electrical power. It didn't quite manage 2000 operations per second from its over 5,000 vacuum tubes. It used mercury delay lines for memory. Forty six were built from 1951-54.

The Univac 1108 came to market in 1964. It used integrated circuit technology, and core memory. It implemented multiprogramming using base and limit registers. Generally, data and instructions were put in separate data banks, sort of an application of Harvard architecture that is used in todays multicore multiprocessors. Double precision floating point was supported. The test-and-set instruction enabled synchronization of the cpu's. Close to 300 1108's were sold.

The Sperry Univac 1100 used semiconductor memory in place of core. It could be had with 3 cpu's and up to 256k words of main memory. The 110x/1100 series used the iconic Uniservo tape drives. The 1004 was a programmable punched-card processing system. It included 961 6-bit character storage in core, and a plug-board for programming. It included a printer. Univac equipment could handle 80-column IBM cards, or their unique 90-column, round-hole cards. The 1108 used an operating systems called Exec II for batch processing. Exec 8 added real time operation, time sharing, and running batch jobs in the background.

The most interesting Univac peripheral was the Fastrand drum storage system. Where IBM drums were clothes-dryer sized and spun about a vertical axis, the Fastrand was very large, and spun about a horizontal axis. The cabinet weighed more than 2 tons, was 6 feet long, and had a glass window along the front – maybe so you could see the bits go by. Its capacity was 22 million 36-bit words, equivalent to 99 megabytes. It spun at 880 rpm. It had 64 read/write heads. Average access time was 92 milliseconds, and data transferred at close to 120 kilobytes per second. Each controller could handle 8 of the drum units.

When my undergraduate University got a Fastrand for it's 1108, it had to be lifted in through the roof of the building. Too big for the elevator.Others

This section is a catch-all for several interesting companies that didn't even get to be dwarfs.

Bendix

Bendix Aviation introduced the refrigerator-sized G-15 computer in 1956. This was a bargain, at around $50,000. The author learned to program this machine in Fortran as an undergraduate. It was tube-based, and used paper tape and a printing terminal. You could program in Fortran, but you had to read the Fortran compiler in from paper tape, then read your program in from paper tape, then punch your compiled program, and read it back in to run it.

G-15. Note the paper tape reader at the top.

Somewhat easier to use was the bigger Bendix G-20. The G-20 was a room-sized mainframe computer circa 1961. It was transistor-based, and used 6 microsecond cycle time core memory. Word size was 32-bits, and parity was included. The machine could have up to 32k words. It supported single and double precision floating point, and a special scaled mode where you could choose the location of the point. The first 63 memory locations were index registers. The G-20 had 110 instructions, and ran with a one megahertz clock.

At Carnegie Institute of Technology in the early 1960's a Bendix G-21 supported the campus computation center. This was a custom dual-processor G-20. The G-21 had an interprocessor interrupt. It was programmed in Algol-20. Besides card input, you could access the machine via 16 remote connections, using Teletypes and dial-up lines at 110 or 300 baud. Playing chess against the machine was popular. The Tech machine also had a custom Philco Scopes system, that were memory-mapped crt displays. A good demo was the "SpaceWar" games, with two players at Philco Scopes consoles. Each saw the other's ship against a star background, and could maneuver and shoot space torpedoes. This was an early video game. It used most of the G-21's capabilities, and user job processing slowed when the scopes were operating.

The G-21 interfaced with a RCA 301 computer in the next room, with a RACE mass storage unit. The Bendix machine had eight magnetic tape drives as well as a paper tape drive. There were two high speed (900 lines per minute) printers, and a low speed (450 lines per minute) one. The card reader was an IBM 1402. An early directory system called AND – Alpha Numeric Directory - handled a user's file needs. Before that, you just managed your program and data as trays of punched cards.

Besides the G-21, the Engineering Lab of the Computation Center has a single processor G-20. The Computer Division of Bendix went to Control Data Corporation in 1963, and the G-15 remained in production.

DEC

Digital Equipment corporation is best known for its minicomputers. But, they did get very large, and resulted in the PDP-10 family, which we can reasonably consider a mainframe. The machines used a 36-bit word. The PDP-10 was popular as a host for time sharing systems, and figured prominently on the early ARPAnet. Compuserve at one time used over 200 PDP-10's in their Data Centers. Before founding Microsoft, Bill Gates and Paul Allen wrote Altair Basic on a PDP-10 at Harvard, using an Intel 8080 microprocessor emulator.

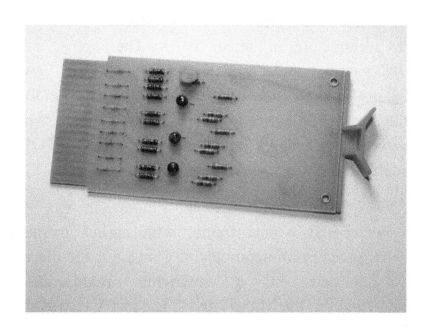

Early DEC discrete component module.

The KA-10 processor unit was initially transistor-based, with unique modules called Flip-chips that fit into backplanes. The backplanes were wire-wrapped. The later KI10 used discrete TTL logic chips, later replaced by faster ECL logic. Later models were microprogrammed. Later cpu models offered paged memory management, and went from 256 kilowords to 4 megawords. Dual CPU models were offered. Original memory was core. There were sixteen general purpose registers. The PDP-10 was discontinued in 1983 in favor of the 32-bit Vax architecture.

VAX defined an instruction set architecture (ISA) for a 32 bit architecture, in the late 1970's. The popular VAX-11/780 was a popular and well-selling model. "VAX" stood for *virtual address extension*, of the PDP-11 architecture. The operating systems was VMS, which was eventually brought into compliance with the POSIX standard. The VAX could run bsd and linux.

The VAX was originally built in ttl logic. The Vax-9000 was considered a mainframe, with earlier members considered super-minicomputers. The VAX architecture was captured in a multichip multiprocessor implementation, the MicroVax-II. The last Vax was built in 2005, but many are still in use.

Philco

Philco Corporation developed the surface barrier transistor in 1953, which gave it an edge in developing high-speed computers. NSA and the Navy asked Philco to build such a machine, and it was produced as the Transac-1000. The Transac-2000 went to the Navy's David Taylor Model Basin in Maryland in 1955. Philco also developed small transistor-based computers for Navy aircraft. The S-1000 and S-2000 were targeted to data processing and scientific computing, respectively. These were the first commercially produced transistor machines. Philco Model 212 computers were used in the Cheyenne Mountain facility of NORAD in 1965. These machines were pipelined, and 4 instructions could be proceeding at once. It used 48-bit words, and had 248 instructions.

Philco 212 at Computer History Museum.

The Philco 2000 in 'the Mountain' generated satellite ephemeris data, to be sent to other installations. This was usually received as IBM card data, which had to be transferred to paper or mylar tape. Later, Philco designed and installed the consoles at NASA-Johnson Space Flight Center's Mission Control. The company went into bankruptcy in 1960, and was acquired by the Ford Motor Company.

Sperry-Rand

Remington Rand was formed in 1927, by the merger of the Remington Typewriter Company, and Rand Cardex, formed by James Rand. Remington originally also manufactured guns, including the M1911A1 model .45 caliber automatic, and electric shavers. In 1950, Remington Rand acquired Eckert-Mauchly Computer, which had been the 1946 commercial venture of the ENIAC builders. Remington-Rand was acquired by Sperry in 1955, and later merged with Burroughs to become Unisys. Remington Typewriter developed the QWERTY keyboard.

Sperry was involved in early computer development for military applications. The Philadelphia Group worked on the one-off Livermore Advanced Research Computer (LARC) supercomputer, while the St. Paul group worked on Navy projects.

The LARC machine was a multiprocessor, with dual cpu's and and a separate I/O processor. The first machine went to the Lawrence Livermore Labs in California in 1960, the second to the Navy's David Taylor Model Basin in Maryland. It was a transistor-based decimal machine, with a 48 bit word. With 4 bits per digit, this gave 11 decimal digit signed numbers. Every digit had a parity bit. The cpu's had 26 general purpose registers, expandable to 99. Each CPU could have up to 24 magnetic drum units for storage, up to forty Univac tape drives, dual printers, and a card reader.

Main memory was implemented in core, to a maximum of just under 100,000 words of 60 bits. There was a data transfer bus linking the CPU's. The core memory had an interlock mechanism to prevent simultaneous access by both cpu's. Each CPU had an add/subtract time of 4 microseconds, a multiplication time of 8, and a divide took 28 microseconds

The Bogart was designed by Sperry Rand in St. Paul, MN for the NSA. It had 4096 words of 24-bit memory, implemented in core. The "small, compact" CPU weighed 3,000 pounds, and covered 20 square feet of floor space. The Bogart design team was headed by Seymour Cray. The prototype was completed in September of 1956. There were four production models built after that. It did not use vacuum tubes to implement logic, but a combination of diodes and magnetic cores, to reduce power. It had 57 instructions for "manipulating data...and performing analytic, counting, and arithmetic operations."

The computer was supposedly named after John B. Bogart, city editor of The New York Sun. This was a reference to the Bogart's primary function - "data editing", what is now called data mining.

At the author's undergraduate university, we had one of these machines, government surplus. We made off with the core memory unit to upgrade another machine, the Athena, mentioned below.

(Reference: Unisys History Newsletter, V3, N4, August 1999. Available at www.silogic.com)

In the late 1950's, missile guidance computers were developed that could adjust the missile's trajectory after launch, but only during power flight. These included the Univac Athena computer for the Air Force's Titan missile system, and the Burroughs Mod 1 for the Atlas missile system. The Smithsonian has one of each computer.

These units were not for flight; they exceeded weight budget by more than 10 tons. The idea of putting the computer on board the vehicle was just a dream at this point.

The Univac Athena required 370 square feet of floor space underground in a hardened bunker. Using radar data input, it calculated course corrections during engine burn. It only had to work for two minutes. It was programmed in assembly language, and was a Harvard architecture, meaning the instructions and data were kept in different stores. In the case of the Athena, the instructions were kept on a magnetic drum, and the data was kept in core.

The Athena cost about $1,800,000. when new, and weighed over 21,000 lbs. The machine was built by Sperry Rand Univac in 1957, with Seymour Cray was the chief designer. It had 256 words of 24-bit core memory for data and a 8192-word drum for program and constants.

The machine had 256 words of 24-bit core memory for data and a 8192-word drum for program and constants. A most interesting feature was Battle Short: In this mode, referred to as "melt-before-fail", the power to the machine could NOT be shut off. Once in service, it was found to have a mean time to failure of 48 days, twenty times better than the original specifications.

The Titan launch complex was located underground, and a single Athena could be used with multiple missiles, launched one at a time. There were eighteen missile complexes, each capable of launching multiple missiles. The liquid-fueled Titan's were considered to be only a stop-gap measure pending the deployment of the solid fuel Minuteman Missile, and none of the complexes were operational for more than four years.

The computer had a Harvard architecture design; separate data and instruction memories were used. A Friedan printing terminal with paper tape equipment was used with the Athena, as well as an operating console.

The Athena used a massive motor-generator set with 440 volt 3 phase AC input. The author hooked this up from the lab mains, and got the generator set going initially. When the generator was started, the building lights dimmed, and there was no question that the machine was on. The motor generator control unit weighed a ton, and the motor/generator itself weighed more than two tons.

Eventually, 23 Athena's were delivered to the Air Force. There were 18 Titan-1 Missile Complexes in the mainland United States. The last launch supported by an Athena computer was a Thor-Agena missile launched in 1972 from Vandenberg AFB in California. The Athena was used on more than 400 missile flights. In its operational life, it never launched a missile in anger.

Athenas were also used to guide Thor missiles launched from Vandenberg AFB and Johnson Island, in the pacific Ocean. The CDC 1600 was used as the targeting computer. These were anti-satellite demonstration launches, using U.S. Target satellites. The target data (orbital ephemeris) was supplied by the Cheyenne Mountain facility, dug into a mountain in Colorado, in the form of punched cards. These were converted to mylar tape on the CDC1600, which was fed into the Athena.

The computers, when declared surplus by the Federal Government, went to various US universities. The one at Carnegie was used as an undergrad project until 1971, when the former EE undergrad students (Athena Systems Development Group) orchestrated its donation to the Smithsonian. It joined a sister unit, the Atlas Mod I Guidance Computer, at the Smithsonian.

The AN/USQ-17 Navy Tactical Data System computer was designed for shipboard use to control radars and direct fire control. It was designed by Seymour Cray right before he departed Sperry for Control Data. In 1957. The processor and memory was reported to be the size of a bathtub. The redesigned units was placed upright, like a refrigerator. The word size was 30 bits. It was built in transistor technology. The four basic math operations were implemented. The cpu had 7 index registers, and 32k words of core. Seventeen units were delivered to the Navy. It was very reliable, with a mean time between failure of more than 100 days. Multiple shipboard computers were linked together. A commercial version was produced, the Univac 1206. In 1963, 94 units were at work for the Navy and NASA.

Sylvania

Sylvania set up its Computer Development section in 1946, to build parts of MIT's Whirlwind project. They did some work on digital cockpit simulators for the Air Force and the Navy.

Sylvania was a bit-player (no pun intended) in computer systems, but did do some unique military units. The Mobile Digital Computer, or MOBIDIC, was a 1956 project for the Army Signal Corps. It was a mobile computer, in the sense that it was mounted in a 30-foot semi-trailer for track transportation. A second truck hauled the 30 kilowatt generator.

The army designation was AN/MYK-1. There was a later dual cpu version. A commercial spinoff was the Sylvania S9400, targeted to factory automation.

The Mobidic was a 36-bit machine. It used core memory in 4k banks, and could support from 2-7. It was one of the first fully transistor-based general purpose cpu's built. It used a Freiden Flexowriter as an operator console. There were 52 instructions; add took 16 microseconds, and multiply, 86. The Mobidic-B had dual processors.

The computer was implemented in transistor technology. The first units was delivered in December, 1959. Four additional machines plus a Cobol compiler were ordered. The units supported the Army's supply and logistics efforts. Tape drives were included. The strength of the machine was its real-time Input-output system.

One of the units made it to the National Bureau of Standards to support research. Later, Sylvania declined to use the architecture of MOBIDIC for the Ballistic Missile Early Warning System (BMEWS), but to work with IBM and their 7090.

From purpose-built one-of-a-kind machines to mass commodities, driven by the needs of commerce, the big mainframe computers got the job done, before they were shrunk to fit on desktops, and later, laptops. There legacy lives on in the computing and computation infrastructure of today.

It is amazing how far computers have come. It will be more amazing to see how far they can go.

Stop reading this book. If you want to see mainframes, go to the Computer History Museum in Mountain View, California. www.computerhistory.org

Better yet, finish reading the book, and then go.

Glossary of Terms and Acronyms

1's complement – a binary number representation scheme for negative values.

2's complement – another binary number representation scheme for negative values.

Accumulator – a register to hold numeric values during and after an operation.

ACM – Association for Computing Machinery; professional organization.

Ada – a programming language named after Ada Augusta, Countess of Lovelace, and daughter of Lord Byron; arguably, the first programmer. Collaborator with Charles Babbage.

AFB – (U.S.) Air Force Base.

AI – artificial intelligence.

Algol – a computer language.

ALU – arithmetic logic unit.

ANSI – American National Standards Institute

ArpaNet – Advanced Research Projects Agency (U.S.), first packet switched network, 1968.

ASCII - American Standard Code for Information Interchange, a 7-bit code; developed for teleprinters.

Assembly language – low level programming language specific to a particular ISA.

Async – asynchronous; using different clocks.

Babbage, Charles –early 19th century inventor of mechanical computing machinery to solve difference equations, and output typeset results; later machines would be fully programmable.

Baudot – code developed by Emile Baudot in 1870 for telegraph use. 5 bit code.

Baud – symbol rate; may or may not be the same as bit rate.

BCD – binary coded decimal. 4-bit entity used to represent 10 different decimal digits; with 6 spare states.

Big-endian – data format with the most significant bit or byte at the lowest address, or transmitted first.

Binary – using base 2 arithmetic for number representation.

BIST – built-in self test.

Bit – smallest unit of digital information; two states.

Blackbox – functional device with inputs and outputs, but no detail on the internal workings.

Boolean – a data type with two values; an operation on these data types; named after George Boole, mid-19th century inventor of Boolean algebra.

Bootstrap – a startup or reset process that proceeds without external intervention.

Bps – bits per second

bsd – Berkeley System Distribution (of Unix)

Buffer – a temporary holding location for data.

Bug – an error in a program or device. Supposedly related to a dead month found jamming a relay in the Harvard Mark-II.

Bus – data channel, communication pathway for data transfer.

Byte – ordered collection of 8 bits; values from 0-255

C – programming language from Bell Labs, circa 1972.

Cache – faster and smaller intermediate memory between the processor and main memory.

Cd – compact disk. An optical media holding about 700 Megabytes.

Chip – integrated circuit component.

Clock – periodic timing signal to control and synchronize operations.

CMOS – complementary metal oxide semiconductor; a technology using both positive and negative semiconductors to achieve low power operation.

Cobol – Common Business oriented language.

Complement – in binary logic, the opposite state.

Compilation – software process to translate source code to assembly or machine code (or error codes).

Control Flow – computer architecture involving directed flow through the program; data dependent paths are allowed.

Coprocessor – another processor to supplement the operations of the main processor. Used for floating point, video, etc. Usually relies on the main processor for instruction fetch; and control.

Core – early non-volatile memory technology based on ferromagnetic toroid's.

Cots – commercial, off-the-shelf.

CPU – central processing unit.

CRAM - card random access memory.

CRT – cathode ray tube. Display technology.

CTSS - Compatible Time Sharing Ssytem.

DARPA – (U. S.) Defense Advanced Research Projects Agency.

Dataflow – computer architecture where a changing value forces recalculation of dependent values.

Deadlock – a situation in which two or more competing actions are each waiting for the other to finish, and thus neither ever does.

DCE – data communications equipment; interface to the network.

Denorm – in floating point representation, a non-zero number with a magnitude less than the smallest normal number.

Device driver – specific software to interface a peripheral to the operating system.

Digital – using discrete values for representation of states or numbers.

Dirty bit – used to signal that the contents of a cache have changed.

DMA - direct memory access (to/from memory, for I/O devices).

Double word – two words; if word = 8 bits, double word = 16 bits.

DTE – data terminal equipment; communicates with the DCE to get to the network.

DVD – digital video disk, optical storage media holding about 4.7 gigabytes.

EBCDIC – an 8-bit character, extended binary coded decimal interchange code, introduced by IBM.

ECL – emitter coupled logic, a fast but power hungry transistor technology.

EIA – Electronics Industry Association.

Epitaxial – in semiconductors, have a crystalline overlayer with a well-defined orientation.

Eprom – erasable programmable read-only memory.

Ethernet – 1980's networking technology. IEEE 802.3.

Exception – interrupt due to internal events, such as overflow.

FET – field effect transistor.

Fetch/execute cycle – basic operating cycle of a computer; fetch the instruction, execute the instruction.

Firmware – code contained in a non-volatile memory.

Fixed point – computer numeric format with a fixed number of digits or bits, and a fixed radix point. Integers.

Flag – a binary indicator.

Flip-flop – a circuit with two stable states; ideal for binary.

Floating point – computer numeric format for real numbers; has significant digits and an exponent.

Fortran – Formula Translation – a scientific programming language.

FPGA – field programmable gate array.

FPU – floating point unit, an ALU for floating point numbers.

Full duplex – communication in both directions simultaneously.

Gate – a circuit to implement a logic function; can have multiple inputs, but a single output.

Giga - 10^9 or 2^{30} (billion).

gigaflop – billion floating point operations per second.

Half-duplex – communications in two directions, but not simultaneously.

Handshake – co-ordination mechanism.

Harvard architecture – memory storage scheme with separate instructions and data.

Hexadecimal – base 16 number representation.

Hexadecimal point – radix point that separates integer from fractional values of hexadecimal numbers.

Hysteresis - in a material or process, the output is dependent not only on the current input, but also the history. A state machine.

IEEE – Institute of Electrical and Electronic Engineers. Professional organization and standards body.

IEEE-754 – standard for floating point representation and operations.

Infinity - the largest number that can be represented in the number system.

Integer – the natural numbers, zero, and the negatives of the natural numbers.

Interrupt – an asynchronous event to signal a need for attention (example: the phone rings).

Interrupt vector – entry in a table pointing to an interrupt service routine; indexed by interrupt number.

I/O – Input-output from the computer to external devices, or a user interface.

ISA – instruction set architecture, the software description of the computer.

ISO – International Standards Organization.

JCL – (IBM) Job Control Language.

Kbytes – kilo bytes (one thousand)

Khz – kilo Hertz (cycles per second).

Kilo – a prefix for 10^3 or 2^{10}

kva – kilo volts-amps, a power measurement.

LAN – local area network.

Latency – time delay.

Linux – free and open source operating system.

LISP – computer language for AI – object-oriented.

Little-endian – data format with the least significant bit or byte at the highest address, or transmitted last.

Logic operation – generally, negate, AND, OR, XOR, and their inverses.

Logosyllabic – a symbolic representation scheme for words, not letters.

LRU – least recently used; an algorithm for item replacement in a cache.

LSB – least significant bit or byte.

LUT – look up table.

Machine language – native code for a particular computer hardware.

Mainframe – a computer you can't lift.

Mantissa – significant digits (as opposed to the exponent) of a floating point value.

Master-slave – control process with one element in charge. Master status may be exchanged among elements.

Math operation – generally, add, subtract, multiply, divide.

Mega - 10^6 or 2^{20}

Microcode – hardware level data structures to translate machine instructions into sequences of circuit level operations. Used to allow one machine to execute the instructions for another, by breaking instructions down into smaller "microcode" units.

Microprocessor – a monolithic cpu on a chip.

MIMD – multiple instruction, multiple data

Minicomputer – smaller than a mainframe, larger than a pc.

MIPS – millions of instructions per second; sometimes used as a measure of throughput.

MMU – memory management unit; translates virtual to physical addresses.

Modem – modulator/demodulator; digital communications interface for analog channels..

MSB – most significant bit or byte.

MSFC – NASA's Marshall Space Flight Center.

Multiplex – combining signals on a communication channel by sampling.

Mutex – a data structure and methodology for mutual exclusion.

NAN – not-a-number; invalid bit pattern.

NAND – negated (or inverse) AND function.

NASA – National Aeronautics and Space Administration.

Nibble – 4 bits, ½ byte.

NIST – National Institute of Standards and Technology (US), previously, National Bureau of Standards.

NOR – negated (or inverse) OR function.

NORAD – North American Aerospace Defense Command.

Normalized number – in the proper format for floating point representation.

NSA – (U.S.) National Security Agency

Null modem – acting as two modems, wired back to back. Artifact of the RS-232 standard.

Octal – base 8 number.

Off-the-shelf – commercially available; not custom.

ONR – (U. S.) Office of Naval Research

Opcode – part of a machine language instruction that specifies the operation to be performed.

Open source – methodology for hardware or software development with free distribution and access.

Operating system – software that controls the allocation of resources in a computer.

Overflow - the result of an arithmetic operation exceeds the capacity of the destination.

Packet – a small container; a block of data on a network.

Paging – memory management technique using fixed size memory blocks.

Paradigm – a pattern or model

Paradigm shift – a change from one paradigm to another. Disruptive or evolutionary.

Parallel – multiple operations or communication proceeding simultaneously.

Parity – an error detecting mechanism involving an extra check bit in the word.

PC – personal computer, politically correct, program counter.

PCB – printed circuit board.

Pinout – mapping of signals to I/O pins of a device.

Pipeline – operations in serial, assembly-line fashion.

Pixel – picture element; smallest addressable element on a display or a sensor.

POSIX – IEEE standard for a Portable Unix-like operating system.

PSW – Program Status Word.

Quad word – four words. If word = 16 bits, quad word is 64 bits.

Queue – first in, first out data buffer structure; hardware of software.

Radix point – separates integer and fractional parts of a real number.

RAM – random access memory; any item can be access in the same time as any other.

Register – temporary storage location for a data item.

Reset – signal and process that returns the hardware to a known, defined state.

ROI - return on investment.

ROM – read only memory.

Real-time – system that responds to events in a predictable, bounded time.

RS-232 – EIA telecommunications standard (1962), serial with handshake.

SAM – sequential access memory, like a magnetic tape.

Sandbox – an isolated and controlled environment to run untested or potentially malicious code.

Self-modifying code – computer code that modifies itself as it run; hard to debug

Semiconductor – material with electrical characteristics between conductors and insulators; basis of current technology processor and memory devices.

Semaphore –signaling element among processes.

Serial – bit by bit.

Server – a computer running services on a network.

Shift – move one bit position to the left or right in a word.

Sign-magnitude – number representation with a specific sign bit.

Signed number – representation with a value and a numeric sign.

SIMD – single instruction, multiple data. Sometimes called a vector processor.

Software – set of instructions and data to tell a computer what to do.

Stack – first in, last out data structure. Can be implemented in hardware of software.

Stack machine – zero address, or zero register machine. All data is on the stack.

Stack pointer – a reference pointer to the top of the stack.

State machine – model of sequential processes.

Synchronous – using the same clock to coordinate operations.

System – a collection of interacting elements and relationships with a specific behavior.

Tera - 10^{12} or 2^{40}

TCP/IP – transmission control protocol/internet protocol; layered set of protocols for networks.

Thread – smallest independent set of instructions managed by a multiprocessing operating system.

Transceiver – receiver and transmitter in one box.

TRAP – exception or fault handling mechanism in a computer; an operating system component.

Truncate – discard. Cutoff, make shorter.

TTL – transistor-transistor logic in digital integrated circuits. (1963).

TWX – teletypewriter exchange, a very early data network.

UART – universal asynchronous receiver-transmitter. Parallel-to-serial; serial-to parallel device with handshaking.

Underflow – the result of an arithmetic operation is smaller than the smallest re-presentable number.

USAF – United States Air Force.

Unsigned number – a number without a numeric sign.

Vector – single dimensional array of values.

Virtual memory – memory management technique using address translation.

Virtualization – creating a virtual resource from available physical resources.

Virus – malignant computer program.

von Neumann – John, a computer pioneer and mathematician; realized that computer instructions are data.

Wiki – the Hawaiian word for "quick." Refers to a collaborative content website.

Williams tube - a CRT type structure for holding ddata

Word – a collection of bits of any size; does not have to be a power of two.

Write-back – cache organization where the data is not written to main memory until the cache location is needed for re-use. .

X86 – Intel -16, -32, 64-bit ISA.

XOR – exclusive OR; either but not both

References

Computer Architecture, General

Alderman, John *Core Memory, A Visual Survey of Computers,* 2007, Chronicle Books, Inc. ISBN-0-8118-5442-6.

Augarten, Stan, *State of the Art*, 1983, Ticknor & Fields, ISBN 0-89919-206-8.

Augarten, Stan, *Bit by Bit, an Illustrated History of Computers,* 1984, Ticknor & Fields, ISBN-0 89919-302-1.

Bell, C. Gordon and Newell, Allen, *Computer Structures: Readings and Examples,* McGraw Hill Inc., January 1, 1971, ISBN- 0070043574.

Blaauw, Gerrit A. and Brooks, Frederick P. Jr. *Computer Architecture, Concepts and Evolution*, 2 volumes, 1997, Addison-Wesley, IBN 0-201-10557-8.

Brooks, Fred, *The Mythical Man-Month,* Addison-Wesley, 1975, ISBN-0-201-00650-2.

Bryant, Randal E. and O'Hallaron, David R. *Computer Systems: A Programmer's Perspective*, 2nd edition, Addison Wesley, ASIN: B004S81RXE.

Boole, George *An Investigation of the Laws of Thought on which are Founded the Mathematical Theories of Logic and Probability*, 1854, reprinted 1958, Dover, ISBN 0-48660028-9.

Burks, Arthur; W. Goldstein, Herman H.; Von Neumann, John *Preliminary Discussion of the Logical Design of an Electronic Computing Instrument*, 1987, MIT Press, originally published in Papers of John Von Neumann on Computing and Computer Theory.

Carter, Nick Schaum's *Outline of Computer Architecture*, McGraw-Hill; 1st edition (December 26, 2001) ISBN-007136207X.

Comer, Douglas E. *Essentials of Computer Architecture*, Prentice Hall; US Ed edition (August 23, 2004) ISBN 0131491792.

Englander, Irv *The Architecture of Computer Hardware and Systems Software: An Information Technology Approach*, Wiley; 3 edition (January 20, 2003) ISBN-0471073253.

Everett, R. R. and Swain, F. E. *Project Whirlwind*, Report R-127, Whirlwind I Computer, Servomechanisms Laboratory, M.I.T., Sept 4,1947.

Flamm, Kenneth, *Creating the Computer: Government, Industry, and High Technology,* 1988, Brookings Institute Press, ISBN-0815728506.

Flores, Ivan *The Logic of Computer Arithmetic,* 1963, Prentice-Hall, ISBN 0135400392.

Goldberg, David *What Every Computer Scientist Should Know About Floating-Point Arithmetic*, March, 1991 issue, Computing Surveys. Copyright 1991, Association for Computing Machinery, Inc.

Goldstein, Gordon D. (ed), Digital Computer Newsletter, Office of Naval Research, Mathematical Sciences Division, Oct. 1985. (Burroughs B8500, Honeywell H-8200, Univac 1830)

Grandy, Anthony *The Early Computer Industry: Limitations of Scale and Scope,* 2012, Palgrave Macmillan, ISBN- 0230389104.

Harris, David and Harris, Sarah *Digital Design and Computer Architecture*, Morgan Kaufmann , 2007, ISBN 012370497.

Heide, Hans, *Punched-Card Systems and the Early Information Explosion*, 1880-1945, 2009, JHU Press, ISBN-0801891434 .

Hennessy, John L. and Patterson, David A. *Computer Architecture, Fifth Edition: A Quantitative Approach*, Morgan Kaufmann; (September 30, 2011) ISBN 012383872X.

Heuring, Vincent, and Jordan, Harry F. *Computer Systems Design and Architecture* (2nd Edition), Prentice Hall; 2 edition (December 6, 2003) ISBN 0130484407.

ANSI/IEEE Standard 754-1985 for Binary Floating-Point Arithmetic, IEEE Computer, Jan. 1980.

IBM Corporation, *IBM System/360 System Summary*, System Reference Library, File S360-00, Form A22-6810-5, 1964.

Kempf, Karl Electronic Computers within the Ordnance Corps, Nov. 1961, Aberdeen Proving Grounds, http://ftp.arl.mil/mike/comphist/61ordnance/index.html

Kidder, Tracy *The Soul of a New Machine*, Back Bay Books, June 2000, ISBN 0316491977.

Mano, M. Morris *Computer System Architecture* (3rd Edition), Prentice Hall; 3rd edition (October 29, 1992) ISBN 0131755633.

Murdocca, Miles J. and Heuring, Vincent *Computer Architecture and Organization: An Integrated Approach*, Wiley (March 16, 2007) ISBN 0471733881.

Nisan, Noam and Schocken, Shimon, *The Elements of Computing Systems: Building a Modern Computer from First Principles*, 2005, MIT Press, ISBN 0262640686.

Null, Linda *The Essentials of Computer Organization And Architecture*, Jones & Bartlett Pub; 2 edition (February 15, 2006) ISBN 0763737690.

Ornstein, Severo M. *Computing in the Middle Ages*, 2002, First Books, ISBN 1-4033-1517-5.

Page, Daniel, *A Practical Introduction to Computer Architecture*, 2009, Springer, ISBN 1848822553.

Patterson, David A and Hennessy, John L. *Computer Organization and Design: The Hardware/Software Interface*, Revised Fourth Edition, Morgan Kaufmann; Nov. 2011 ISBN 0123744938.

Quatse, Jesse T. *Design of the G-21 Multi-Processor System,* Carnegie Institute of Technology, Computation Center, Feb. 26, 1965.

Ramachandran, Umakishore, and Leahy William D. Jr., *Computer Systems: An Integrated Approach to Architecture and Operating Systems*, 2010, Addison Wesley, ISBN 0321486137.

Reid, T. R. *The Chip: How Two Americans Invented the Microchip and Launched a Revolution*, Random House Trade Paperbacks; Revised edition (October 9, 2001) ISBN 0375758283.

Richards, R. K. *Arithmetic Operations in Digital Computers, 1955, Van Nostrand,* B00128Z00.

Schmid, Hermann *Decimal Computation*, 1974, Wiley, ISBN 0-471-76180-X.

Silc, Jurji, Robic, Borut, Ungerer, Theo *Processor Architecture: From Dataflow to Superscalar and Beyond*, Springer; 1st edition (July 20, 1999) ISBN 3540647988.

Smotherman, Mark, *IBM Advanced Computing Systems (ACS) – 1961-1969.*, http://people.cs.clemson.edu/~mark/acs.html

Stallings, William *Computer Organization and Architecture: Designing for Performance* (7th Edition), Prentice Hall; 7 edition (July 21, 2005) ISBN 0131856448.

von Neumann, John *First Draft of a Report on the EDVAC,* 1945, avail: http://systemcomputing.org/turing %20award/Maurice_1967/TheFirstDraft.pdf

Wilkes, M. V. *Automatic Digital Computers*, 1956, Wiley.(revised edition, 1957, ASIN- B0007IX5WU.

Burroughs References

Parts Manual for Model G-15D Computer, Control Data Corp, Publication 60061400,

DA-1 Differential analyzer for the Control Data G-15 Computer, Service Manual, Publication 60064800, May 1965, Control Data Corporation.

Theory of Operation & Simplified Drawings for Control Data G-15 Computer, 1964, Publication 60121600.

Programming for the G-15, 4 parts, Bendix Corporation, Computer Division, 1960, APR-01601.

Bendix G-20 General Reference Manual, Bendix Corporation, Computer Division, 1962, BER-05624.

G-20 Central Processor Service Manual Vol 1 & 2, BER-10622.

Bendix G-20, Peripheral Equipment Machine Language, BET-12611.

G15D Technical Manual, Revision 1, parts 1, 2, 3, Bendix Computer, Division of Bendix Aviation Corporation.

Bendix G-20 Central Processor Machine Language, Bendix Corporation, T23-1.

Sperry Rand References

Instruction Book for Bogart Computing System, Navy Model CXPX, 12 volumes, December 1957, Remington

Rand Univac, Dept. of the Navy, Bureau of Ships, Contract NObsr 63010, Task 39.

Sage References

http://bitsavers.trailing-edge.com/pdf/ibm/sage/SAGE_BOMARC_Defense_Syst em_1958.pdf

http://www.computermuseum.li/Testpage/IBM-SAGE-computer.htm

http://bitsavers.informatik.uni-stuttgart.de/pdf/ibm/sage/22-00001_Central_Computer_System_Preliminary_Sep55.p df

http://www.mitre.org/about/photo_archives/sage_photo.h tml

Astrahan, Morton M.; Jacobs, John F. (1983). "History of the Design of the SAGE Computer - The AN/FSQ-7". Annals of the History of Computing (IEEE) 5 (4): 340–349.

http://www.livinginternet.com/i/ii_sage.htm

Redmond, Kent C., Smith, Thomas M. *From Whirlwind to MITRE: The R&D Story of The SAGE Air Defense Computer* (History of Computing), MIT Press, October 16, 2000, ISBN- 0262182017.

IBM S/360 References

http://www-03.ibm.com/ibm/history/exhibits/mainframe/mainframe_PP2075.html

IBM Systems Journal Vol. 23 No 3 1984 pgs 245-255.

http://www-03.ibm.com/ibm/history/exhibits/mainframe/mainframe_PP2075.html

IBM System/360 Timesharing (TSS)

C28-2024-2   Manager's and Administrator's Guide

C28-2002-0 Command Language for Administrators and Operators

          User Manual

C28-2017-1 Terminal User's Guide

C28-2025-0 Fortran Programmer's Guide

C28-2033-1 Operator's Guide

          Task Monitor Introduction

          Task Monitor

          VSAM Record Formats

Linkage Editor

C28-2010-4 System Generation and Maintenance

S360-25   Fortran Programmer Guide Amendments, 12/15/67

C28-2043-6 Addendum

C28-2001-4 Command System User's Guide

C28-2000-2 Assembly Language

S360-21   Assembly Language, Addendum 12/15/67

TSS/360   Technical Newsletter, POD? Command

TSS User Manual for Carnegie Mellon University User   community

A Fortran Programmer's Introduction to the Use of TSS/360,   June 1968

TSS/360 Compendium

C28-2003-2 Concepts and Facilities

IBM TSS/360 User Manual, July 1, 1969.

IBM System/360 Model 67 Functional characteristics, A27-2719-0, 1967.

A22-6898-0 IBM System/360 Model 50 Functional Characteristics

IBM System/360 Instruction Timing Information, A22-6825-1, May 1964.

IBM System/360 System Summary, A22-6810-10, Nov. 3, 1969.

IBM Customer Engineering Manual of Instruction, Transistor Component Circuits, 1963.

CDC References

http://bitsavers.informatik.uni-stuttgart.de/pdf/cdc/924/

RCA References

TP1134_RCA110_PrgmRef_Aug62.pdf.
http://bitsavers.trailing-edge.com/pdf/rca/110/

RCA, RCA 110 Computer, Programmer's Reference Manual, August 1962, TP-1134

Resources

www.silogic.com

http://www-03.ibm.com/ibm/history/documents/index.html

Many mainframe computer manuals can be found at: http://www.bitsavers.org/pdf/

The GE-625/635 Programming Reference Manual is here: http://ed-thelen.org/comp-hist/GE-635.html

http://ftp.arl.army.mil/~mike/comphist/

wikipedia, various.

http://www.computerhistory.org/collections/search/

http://vipclubmn.org/Computers.html

If you enjoyed this book, you might also be interested in some of these.

Stakem, Patrick H. *16-bit Microprocessors, History and Architecture*, 2013 PRRB Publishing, ISBN-1520210922.

Stakem, Patrick H. *4- and 8-bit Microprocessors, Architecture and History*, 2013, PRRB Publishing, ISBN-152021572X,

Stakem, Patrick H. *Apollo's Computers,* 2014, PRRB Publishing, ISBN-1520215800.

Stakem, Patrick H. *The Architecture and Applications of the ARM Microprocessors,* 2013, PRRB Publishing, ISBN-1520215843.

Stakem, Patrick H. *Earth Rovers: for Exploration and Environmental Monitoring,* 2014, PRRB Publishing, ISBN-152021586X.

Stakem, Patrick H. *Embedded Computer Systems, Volume 1, Introduction and Architecture*, 2013, PRRB Publishing, ISBN-1520215959.

Stakem, Patrick H. *The History of Spacecraft Computers from the V-2 to the Space Station*, 2013, PRRB Publishing, ISBN-1520216181.

Stakem, Patrick H. *Floating Point Computation*, 2013, PRRB Publishing, ISBN-152021619X.

Stakem, Patrick H. *Architecture of Massively Parallel Microprocessor Systems*, 2011, PRRB Publishing, ISBN-1520250061.

Stakem, Patrick H. *Multicore Computer Architecture,* 2014, PRRB Publishing, ISBN-1520241372.

Stakem, Patrick H. *Personal Robots*, 2014, PRRB Publishing, ISBN-1520216254.

Stakem, Patrick H. *RISC Microprocessors, History and Overview,* 2013, PRRB Publishing, ISBN-1520216289.

Stakem, Patrick H. *Robots and Telerobots in Space Application*s, 2011, PRRB Publishing, ISBN-1520210361.

Stakem, Patrick H. *The Saturn Rocket and the Pegasus Missions, 1965,* 2013, PRRB Publishing, ISBN-1520209916.

Stakem, Patrick H. *Visiting the NASA Centers, and Locations of Historic Rockets & Spacecraft,* 2017, PRRB Publishing, ISBN-1549651205.

Stakem, Patrick H. *Microprocessors in Space*, 2011, PRRB Publishing, ISBN-1520216343.

Stakem, Patrick H. *Computer Virtualization and the Cloud*, 2013, PRRB Publishing, ISBN-152021636X.

Stakem, Patrick H. *What's the Worst That Could Happen? Bad Assumptions, Ignorance, Failures and Screw-ups in Engineering Projects, 2014,* PRRB Publishing, ISBN-1520207166.

Stakem, Patrick H. *Computer Architecture & Programming of the Intel x86 Family, 2013,* PRRB Publishing, ISBN-1520263724.

Stakem, Patrick H. *The Hardware and Software Architecture of the Transputer*, 2011,PRRB Publishing, ISBN-152020681X.

Stakem, Patrick H. *Mainframes, Computing on Big Iron*, 2015, PRRB Publishing, ISBN- 1520216459.

Stakem, Patrick H. *Spacecraft Control Centers*, 2015, PRRB Publishing, ISBN-1520200617

Stakem, Patrick H. *Embedded in Space,* 2015, PRRB Publishing, ISBN-1520215916.

Stakem, Patrick H. *A Practitioner's Guide to RISC Microprocessor Architecture*, Wiley-Interscience, 1996, ISBN-0471130184.

Stakem, Patrick H. *Cubesat Engineering*, PRRB Publishing, 2017, ISBN-1520754019.

Stakem, Patrick H. *Cubesat Operations*, PRRB Publishing, 2017, ISBN-152076717X.

Stakem, Patrick H. *Interplanetary Cubesats*, PRRB Publishing, 2017, ISBN-1520766173 .

Stakem, Patrick H. Cubesat Constellations, Clusters, and Swarms, Stakem, PRRB Publishing, 2017, ISBN-1520767544.

Stakem, Patrick H. *Graphics Processing Units, an overview*, 2017, PRRB Publishing, ISBN-1520879695.

Stakem, Patrick H. *Intel Embedded and the Arduino-101, 2017,* PRRB Publishing, ISBN-1520879296.

Stakem, Patrick H. *Orbital Debris, the problem and the mitigation*, 2018, PRRB Publishing, ISBN-*1980466483.*

Stakem, Patrick H. *Manufacturing in Space*, 2018, PRRB Publishing, ISBN-1977076041.

Stakem, Patrick H. *NASA's Ships and Planes*, 2018, PRRB Publishing, ISBN-1977076823.

Stakem, Patrick H. *Space Tourism*, 2018, PRRB Publishing, ISBN-1977073506.

Stakem, Patrick H. *STEM – Data Storage and Communications*, 2018, PRRB Publishing, ISBN-1977073115.

Stakem, Patrick H. *In-Space Robotic Repair and Servicing*, 2018, PRRB Publishing, ISBN-1980478236.

Stakem, Patrick H. *Introducing Weather in the pre-K to 12 Curricula, A Resource Guide for Educators*, 2017, PRRB Publishing, ISBN-1980638241.

Stakem, Patrick H. *Introducing Astronomy in the pre-K to 12 Curricula, A Resource Guide for Educators*, 2017, PRRB Publishing, ISBN-198104065X.

Also available in a Brazilian Portuguese edition, ISBN-1983106127.

Stakem, Patrick H. *Deep Space Gateways, the Moon and Beyond*, 2017, PRRB Publishing, ISBN-1973465701.

Stakem, Patrick H. *Exploration of the Gas Giants, Space Missions to Jupiter, Saturn, Uranus, and Neptune*, PRRB Publishing, 2018, ISBN-9781717814500.

Stakem, Patrick H. *Crewed Spacecraft*, 2017, PRRB Publishing, ISBN-1549992406.

Stakem, Patrick H. *Rocketplanes to Space*, 2017, PRRB Publishing, ISBN-1549992589.

Stakem, Patrick H. *Crewed Space Stations,* 2017, PRRB Publishing, ISBN-1549992228.

Stakem, Patrick H. *Enviro-bots for STEM: Using Robotics in the pre-K to 12 Curricula, A Resource Guide for Educators,* 2017, PRRB Publishing, ISBN-1549656619.

Stakem, Patrick H. *STEM-Sat, Using Cubesats in the pre-K to 12 Curricula, A Resource Guide for Educators*, 2017, ISBN-1549656376.

Stakem, Patrick H. *Lunar Orbital Platform-Gateway*, 2018, PRRB Publishing, ISBN-1980498628.

Stakem, Patrick H. *Embedded GPU's*, 2018, PRRB Publishing, ISBN- 1980476497.

Stakem, Patrick H. *Mobile Cloud Robotics*, 2018, PRRB Publishing, ISBN- 1980488088.

Stakem, Patrick H. *Extreme Environment Embedded Systems,* 2017, PRRB Publishing, ISBN-1520215967.

Stakem, Patrick H. *What's the Worst, Volume-2*, 2018, ISBN-1981005579.

Stakem, Patrick H., *Spaceports*, 2018, ISBN-1981022287.

Stakem, Patrick H., *Space Launch Vehicles*, 2018, ISBN-1983071773.

Stakem, Patrick H. *Mars*, 2018, ISBN-1983116902.

Stakem, Patrick H. *X-86, 40th Anniversary ed*, 2018, ISBN-1983189405.

Stakem, Patrick H. *Lunar Orbital Platform-Gateway*, 2018, PRRB Publishing, ISBN-1980498628.

Stakem, Patrick H. *Space Weather*, 2018, ISBN-1723904023.

Stakem, Patrick H. *STEM-Engineering Process*, 2017, ISBN-1983196517.

Stakem, Patrick H. *Space Telescopes,* 2018, PRRB Publishing, ISBN-1728728568.

Stakem, Patrick H. *Exoplanets*, 2018, PRRB Publishing, ISBN-9781731385055.

Stakem, Patrick H. *Planetary Defense*, 2018, PRRB Publishing, ISBN-9781731001207.

Patrick H. Stakem *Exploration of the Asteroid Belt*, 2018, PRRB Publishing, ISBN-1731049846.

Patrick H. Stakem *Terraforming*, 2018, PRRB Publishing, ISBN-1790308100.

Patrick H. Stakem, *Martian Railroad,* 2019, PRRB Publishing, ISBN-1794488243.

Patrick H. Stakem, *Exoplanets,* 2019, PRRB Publishing, ISBN-1731385056.

Patrick H. Stakem, *Exploiting the Moon,* 2019, PRRB Publishing, ISBN-1091057850.

Patrick H. Stakem, *RISC-V, an Open Source Solution for Space Flight Computers,* 2019, PRRB Publishing, ISBN-1796434388.

Patrick H. Stakem, *Arm in Space*, 2019, PRRB Publishing, ISBN-9781099789137.

Patrick H. Stakem, *Extraterrestrial Life*, 2019, PRRB Publishing, ISBN-978-1072072188.

Patrick H. Stakem, *Space Command*, 2019, PRRB Publishing, ISBN-978-1693005398.

CubeRovers, A Synergy of Technologys, 2020, PRRB Publishing, ISBN-979-8651773138.

Robotic Exploration of the Icy moons of the Gas Giants. 2020, PRRB Publishing, ISBN- 979-8621431006

Hacking Cubesats, 2020, PRRB Publishing, ISBN-979-8623458964.

History & Future of Cubesats, PRRB Publishing, ISBN-979-8649179386.

Hacking Cubesats, Cybersecurity in Space, 2020, PRRB Publishing, ISBN-979-8623458964.

Powerships, Powerbarges, Floating Wind Farms: electricity when and where you need it, 2021, PRRB Publishing, ISBN-979-8716199477.

Hospital Ships, Trains, and Aircraft, 2020, PRRB Publishing, ISBN-979-8642944349.

2020/2021 Releases

CubeRovers, a Synergy of Technologys, 2020, ISBN-979-8651773138

Exploration of Lunar & Martian Lava Tubes by Cube-X, ISBN-979-8621435325.

History & Future of Cubesats, ISBN-978-1986536356.

Robotic Exploration of the Icy Moons of the Ice Giants, by Swarms of Cubesats, ISBN-979-8621431006.

Swarm Robotics, ISBN-979-8534505948.

Introduction to Electric Power Systems, ISBN-979-8519208727.

Centros de Control: Operaciones en Satélites del Estándar CubeSat (Spanish Edition), 2021, ISBN-979-8510113068.

Exploration of Venus, 2022, ISBN-979-8484416110.

Patrick H. Stakem, *The Search for Extraterrestial Life,* 2019, PRRB Publishing, ISBN-1072072181.

The Artemis Missions, Return to the Moon, and on to Mars, 2021, ISBN-979-8490532361.

James Webb Space Telescope. A New Era in Astronomy, 2021, ISBN-979-8773857969.

www.ingramcontent.com/pod-product-compliance
Lightning Source LLC
LaVergne TN
LVHW092333060326
832902LV00008B/615